**Benjamin Weyers, Nelson Baloian,
Wolfram Luther (Eds.)**

Ambient Intelligence in Metropolitan Regions

**International Workshop SADUE13 at the University of Chile,
August 26 to August 30, 2013**

Revised contributions

Volume Editors

Benjamin Weyers
RWTH Aachen University
Virtual Reality Group
Seffenter Weg 23, 52074 Aachen, Germany
E-mail: weyers@vr.rwth-aachen.de

Nelson Baloian
Department of Computer Science, Universidad de Chile
Blanco Encalada 2120, Santiago 6511224, Chile
E-mail: nbaloian@dcc.uchile.cl

Wolfram Luther
University of Duisburg-Essen,
Department of Computer Science and Applied Cognitive Science
Lotharstraße 63, 47048 Duisburg, Germany
E-mail: luther@inf.uni-due.de

ACM Subject Classification (1998): H.1.2, H.5.1. H.5.2, I.6.4, J.1, K.4
ISBN 978-3-8325-3643-5
Logos Verlag Berlin

PREFACE

After three international summer academies funded by the German Academic Exchange Service (DAAD) at universities in Chile (Universidad de Chile UCH, Pontificia Universidad Católica de Chile) in 2008, Germany (University of Duisburg-Essen UDE) in 2009, and Japan (WASEDA University, University of Tokushima) in 2010, attendees decided to step up their cooperation by identifying a common research topic relevant in today's computer science research: *Ambient Intelligence in Metropolitan Regions (AIMR)*. As a starting point for a DFG-funded scientific network, these young researchers got together with their former doctoral advisors and their associated doctoral students at the Universidad de Chile for the SADUE workshop in August 2013. This volume is a collection of the original material presented by the lecturers and summarizes the research work presented at the workshop.

The first presentation was held by *Wolfram Luther*. In it, he discussed our goals and motivations for coming together once more, introduced the thematic orientation of the workshop, explained its relationship to work done at the summer academies, and commented on the intended sustainability of the workshop results. It is hoped that these results will motivate young researchers to continue to their collaboration in a research network.

The succeeding talks in this volume are organized thematically. The first set focuses on collaborative systems. *Nelson Baloian* and *Gustavo Zurita* present a design for situated learning applications using cloud services, *Valeria Herskovic* and her colleagues discuss collaboration in healthcare, *José Pino* and his team highlight business process elicitation in mobile collaboration environments with an agile methodology, *Álvaro Monares* presents the use of unconventional awareness mechanisms to support mobile work, and *Francisco Gutierrez* highlights research in partially virtual communities.

The topic of human computer interaction in AIMR is covered by *Benjamin Weyers'* talk, entitled "Ambient Intelligence in Metropolitan Regions: A User Interface Perspective."

The next three presentations examine context awareness and ubiquitous computing. First, *Tim Hussein* discusses his work on critique-based context-aware recommendation in metropolitan regions. Then, *Daniel Moreno Córdova* and *Sergio Ochoa* present a context-aware positioning model for supporting ubiquitous applications. Finally, *Ochoa* gives a brief summary of current projects in mobile and ubiquitous computing.

The next section treats cultural heritage and virtual museums. It comprises talks by *Daniel Biella* and *Daniel Sacher* presenting their work on virtual museums.

Then, *Song Liu* discusses challenges and chances in energy management systems.

The final section, "Reliable Computing and Uncertainty," includes three contributions: *Luther* discusses reliable computing in modeling and simulation software, *Gabor Rebner* explores probabilistic models with uncertainty, and *Jonathan Frez* and his colleagues consider the building of suitability maps using incomplete and uncertain context information.

The organizers, Wolfram Luther (UDE) and Nelson Baloian (UCH), would like to express their gratitude to the German Research Foundation (DFG) for funding the workshop.

Finally, we want to thank all workshop participants for their presentations and contributions to the proceedings.

Aachen, Duisburg, and Santiago, December 2013

The Editors: Benjamin Weyers, Wolfram Luther, and Nelson Baloian

CONTENTS

Workshop SADUE13
Ambient Intelligence in Metropolitan Regions AIMR

Santiago de Chile
August 27-31, 2013

Wolfram Luther
Department of Computer Science and Applied Cognitive Science
University of Duisburg-Essen
luther@inf.uni-due.de

Abstract. This presentation offers an overview of the program and results of the workshop SADUE 13 Ambient Intelligence in Metropolitan Regions AIMR organized by the universities of Duisburg-Essen and Chile with the support of the German Research Foundation (DFG).

Furthermore, the expanded version of the workshop presentation "Reliable Computing in Modeling and Simulating Software" outlines new software tools developed in projects funded by the DFG and EU Ziel 2 program with special emphasis on accurate results despite uncertainty in the model parameters.

Keywords: Accurate modeling and simulation systems, Numerical verification, Assessment, Validation, Uncertainty

1 Organizers

- Prof. Nelson Baloian
  o Department of Computer Sciences (DCC)
  o FCFM (Faculty of Physical and Mathematical Sciences), Universidad de Chile (UCH)
- Prof. Wolfram Luther
  o Department of Computer Science and Applied Cognitive Science (INKO)
  o Faculty of Engineering, University of Duisburg-Essen (UDE)

2 Context

- Cooperation UCH-UDE 1997–2013
- SADUEWA 2008-2010
- CoSMICS AI 2010 (not funded by the DAAD)
  o Doctoral school in Applied Computer Science. Modeling, analyzing, implementing and evaluating interactive and collaborative systems with applications in bio- and geo-informatics, environmental informatics. (CoSMICS-AI)
- PRASEDEC 2013 - 2016
  o Practice-driven Advance of Studies and Exchange between the University of Duisburg-Essen and the University of Chile

3 Recent Common Interests

- Semantic technologies for interactive and learning support systems, learning and training scenarios integrating mobile and ubiquitous computing components using GPS and mobile technology
- Knowledge management and decision–making systems, GIS-based information management systems for environmental modeling under uncertainty
- Analytical information systems assisting users in performing various analyses, such as traffic simulation systems, security, assistance
- Collaboration technologies and systems, distributed human-machine systems with situation-based optimal work distribution to agents and operators, evaluation of CSCW systems from several perspectives
- Ambient assisted living applications
- User interface adaptation based on external context factors, user models, and interaction context, assessing the impact of fixed and reconfigurable displays on distributed situation awareness and mental workload

4 SADUE13 topics

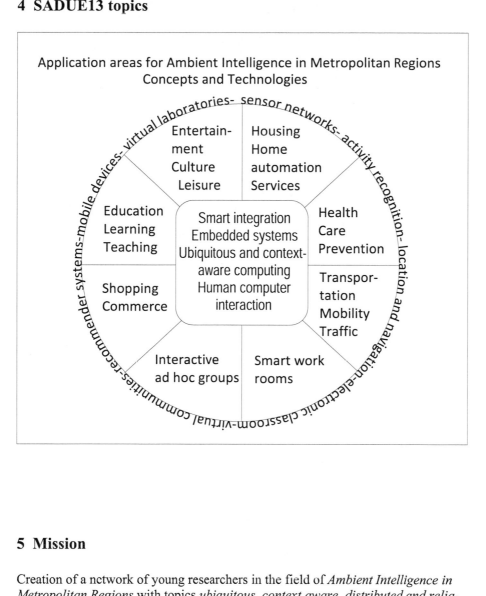

Application areas for Ambient Intelligence in Metropolitan Regions
Concepts and Technologies

virtual laboratories- sensor networks- activity recognition- location and navigation- electronic classroom- virtual communities- recommender systems- mobile devices-

Entertain-ment Culture Leisure	Housing Home automation Services
Education Learning Teaching	Health Care Prevention
Shopping Commerce	Transpor-tation Mobility Traffic
Interactive ad hoc groups	Smart work rooms

Smart integration
Embedded systems
Ubiquitous and context-aware computing
Human computer interaction

5 Mission

Creation of a network of young researchers in the field of *Ambient Intelligence in Metropolitan Regions* with topics *ubiquitous, context aware, distributed and reliable computing*

Who? Professors and researchers already working together in SADUEWA

Where? The metropolitan regions Rhine-Ruhr and SdC

Funded by the DFG, the DAAD and the National Commission for Scientific and Technological Research, Chile (CONICYT)

6 Scientific Networks for Young Researchers (DFG)

- Common research field and "identifiable product" as result
- Software/tool, exhibition, book, e-book, conference series
- Funding of travel, accommodation, meetings, workshop guests, and publications for three years
- 6–15 persons, a third from outside Germany
- http://www.dfg.de/formulare/1_19/1_19_en.pdf

7 Guest Speakers

Prof. Wolfram Luther, University of Duisburg-Essen, INKO
luther@inf.uni-due.de

Dr. Daniel Biella, University of Duisburg-Essen, Center for Information and Media Services (CIM)
daniel.biella@uni-due.de

Dr. Tim Hussein, University of Duisburg-Essen, INKO
tim.hussein@uni-due.de

Dr. Benjamin Weyers, University of Duisburg-Essen, INKO
weyers@inf.uni-due.de, weyers@vr.rwth-aachen.de

Dr. Gabor Rebner, University of Duisburg-Essen, INKO
rebner@inf.uni-due.de

Daniel Sacher, University of Duisburg-Essen, INKO
sacher@inf.uni-due.de

Prof. Song Liu, North China Electric Power University, Peking
liusongjp@gmail.com (via Skype)

8 Chilean Speakers

Prof. Nelson Baloian, University of Chile, DCC
nbaloian@dcc.uchile.cl

Prof. Sergio Ochoa, University of Chile, DCC
sochoa@dcc.uchile.cl

Prof. José Pino, University of Chile, DCC

jpino@dcc.uchile.cl

Prof. Valeria Herskovic, Pontificia Catholic University of Chile, Computer Science Department
vherskov@ing.puc.cl

Prof. Andres Neyem, Pontificia Catholic University of Chile, Computer Science Department
aneyem@ing.puc.cl

9 PhD Students

Jonathan Frez, University of Chile, DCC Avenida Blanco Encalada N° 2120 Santiago Chile
jonathan.frez@gmail.com

Francisco Gutierrez, University of Chile, DCC
frgutier@dcc.uchile.cl

Alvaro Monares, University of Chile, DCC
amonares@dcc.uchile.cl

Daniel Moreno, University of Chile, DCC
dmoreno@dcc.uchile.cl

Carolina Fuentes, Pontificia Catholic University of Chile
cjfuentes@uc.cl

Cecilia Saint-Pierre, Pontificia Catholic University of Chile
csaintpierre@uc.cl

10 Lectures

Prof. Nelson Baloian: Taking Advantage of Cloud Services for Implementing Situated Learning Collaborative Activities

Dr. Daniel Biella: Cultural Heritage in Metropolitan Areas Using a Virtual Museum Framework

Jonathan Frez: Spatial Decision Support Systems & Fuzzy Modeling & Belief Functions

Carolina Fuentes: Human Computer Interfaces to Express and Share Caregivers' Emotional Information

Francisco Gutierrez: Doing Research in Partially Virtual Communities

Prof. Valeria Herskovic: Collaboration Visualization for Application Design

Dr. Tim Hussein: Towards Critique-Based Context-Aware Recommendation in Metropolitan Regions

Prof. Wolfram Luther: Reliable Computing in Modeling and Simulating Software

Alvaro Monares: Unconventional Awareness Mechanics

Daniel Moreno: A Context-Aware Positioning Model to Support Ubiquitous Applications

Prof. Andres Neyem: LiveANDES: Preserving Biodiversity

Prof. Sergio Ochoa: Mobile and Ubiquitous Computing: A Brief Summary of the Current Projects

Prof. José Pino: Mobile Collaboration for Business Process Elicitation from Agile Development Methodology Viewpoint

Gabor Rebner: Verified Mathematical Methods for Computing Stochastic Models with Uncertainty

Daniel Sacher: Virtual Museum Exhibitions: From Content Creation to Presentation

Cecilia Saint-Pierre: Using Process Mining in Electronic Medical Records

Dr. Benjamin Weyers: AIMR: A User Interface Perspective

Prof. Song Liu: Challenges and Chances: Smart Grids (via Skype from China)

11 Organizational Issues

Panel: Baloian, Biella, Herskovic, Hussein, Luther, Neyem, Ochoa, Pino, Weyers
- International network of young researchers – Concept and proposal realization
- Initial coordination meeting of the young researcher group scheduled for Tuesday morning
- SADUE 13 Workshop proceedings
- Slides with introductory text and focus on AIMR, by November, 20 – 3 slides / page – Style sheets
- Proposal
  o Aims

- o Persons, e.g., 4 + 2
- o Activities / Meetings (Intention, guests)
- o Deadline: End of 2013
- o Cosponsoring by Conicyt – PhD students
- o Product: Open-ended e-book concerning AIWR
- To define thematic horizon
  - o New way of publishing – creating and reviewing – executable paper
  - o Interactive book
  - o Bi-annual workshop at **UCAmI & IWAAL & CLIHC**

12 Schedule

	Wednesday Aug. 28	Thursday Aug. 29	Friday Aug. 30
9-10		Weyers	Liu (skype) Pino
10-11		Frez Monares	Gutiérrez Moreno
11:30-12:30		Rebner Sacher	Neyem
12:30-13:30		Lunch	Luis von Ahn (Auditorio Gorbea)
13:30-14:30	Preparation meeting	Baloian Zurita	Ochoa
14:30-15:15	Opening: Baloian Luther		Panel & Programm discussion
15:30-16:30	Biella	Herskovic	
16:30-17:30	Hussein	Fuentes, Saint-Pierre	
18:00-20:00		Reception at DCC	

Implementing Situated Learning Applications Using Cloud Services

Nelson Baloian[1], Gustavo Zurita[2]
[1] Department of Computer Science, Universidad de Chile
nbaloian@dcc.uchile.cl
[2] Management Control and Information Systems Department, Universidad de Chile
gzurita@fen.uchile.cl

Abstract. For situated learning, the context in which learning takes place is of paramount importance. It has been therefore frequently associated with informal learning or learning outside the classroom. Cloud technologies can play an important role in supporting this type of learning since it requires ubiquitous computing support, connectivity, and access to data across various scenarios: in the field, in the classroom, at home, etc. Some of the main characteristics of cloud computing are reliability, scalability, and ubiquity. This makes it especially suitable for supporting large groups performing learning activities that require computer support in various settings both inside and outside the classroom. In this study, we first analyze the use of Google Maps for supporting a learning activity with these characteristics and conclude that some important features are missing. We then propose an approach for taking advantage of cloud computing services for learning activities by integrating different services offered by the cloud in a new application. Finally, we present a general architecture explaining this approach and a sample design for this type of application.

Keywords: collaborative learning, cloud services, software architecture.

1 Introduction

The situated learning theory states that learning requires theoretical concepts learned inside the classroom to be linked to practical situations in authentic contexts where they can be applied [1, 2]. The way in which humans learn implies practicing the concepts acquired in theory [3]. Moreover, teaching and learning activities involving conceptual knowledge (learned inside a classroom), and practical implementation (in real situations) are not only complementary, but also provide reciprocal feedback in a process of ongoing and increasing interaction.

Recent advancements in mobile, wireless, and positioning technologies, combined with contextual computing, provide an opportunity for curricular development that may take advantage of these devices for supporting different aspects of learning and teaching [4]. Mobile and wireless technologies allow interaction with the real world in new ways because computational power and interaction are available outside the boundaries of the classroom. Mobile technologies provide access to content virtually anywhere and anytime, allowing learners to have new learning experiences in a variety of situations beyond those provided in the classroom itself [5, 6].

Nowadays, new learning situations have been proposed that are marked by a continuity of learning experiences across different learning contexts. Students, individually or in groups, carry out learning activities whenever they want in a variety of situations and switch from one scenario to another easily and quickly. In these learning situations, learners are able to examine the physical world by capturing sensor and geo-positional data and conducting scientific inquiries and analyses in new ways that incorporate many of the important characteristics suggested by situated learning

In the literature, we see a growing number of applications developed to support collaborative learning as recommended in the situated learning theory that also make use of geo-referenced information. These applications are also alike in that they implement communication mechanisms that allow learners to interact among themselves and sometimes with the teacher in synchronous or asynchronous ways; thus, they can work collaboratively across various learning situations as well as locations and devices. However, these applications are seldom related to the concepts of grid or cloud computing, nor do they take advantage of what these paradigms can offer. Cloud computing is about ubiquity, reliability, scalability, and cost efficiency, which matches the requirements for applications in which users will be using a variety of devices in different settings and scenarios.

Cloud services are cloud computing functionalities that are accessible via the Internet through a Website "as is" or through an application program interface (API). In this paper, we explore the role of cloud services in supporting new forms of technology-enhanced learning activities. We explore the common understanding of cloud computing, transferring the abstracted features to other prominent Internet services such as Twitter and Facebook (which, for the purposes of this paper, we see as specific instances of cloud services). We argue that, in the context of learning scenarios, a wider definition of cloud services is needed in order to encompass potentially relevant new developments. Furthermore, we present an architecture that allows the flexible use of functionalities that fall within this extended definition. We describe two examples of learning scenarios that built using the architecture presented to demonstrate how these services facilitate innovative technology-enhanced learning scenarios. To conclude, we will examine possible future developments within this understanding of cloud services.

Cloud computing, in all its modalities, is increasingly being used to support collaborative learning activities, especially large groups [7], since scalability is one of its most prominent characteristics.

According to [8], because cloud-based services are accessible from any device connected to the Internet, including desktop PCs, laptops, tablets, and smartphones, using cloud computing to support learning provides cost savings, flexible IT management, and accessible IT resources and services.

On the other hand, it also involves some risks regarding reliability, control, security and privacy, and organizational learning. Vendors of cloud services will never provide 100% reliability. Moreover, the services reside with and are controlled by the vendor. This lack of control also may lead to the risk of security or privacy breaches. Finally, users of cloud services (students and teachers) may need to learn new ways to interact with the software, which may affect organizational learning. In [9] the authors warn that public clouds may offer low-cost services, but in return they may not provide needed assurances of security for those services. They also point out that software as a service (SaaS) often needs to be customized to meet customers' needs. However, providers cannot afford to develop and maintain a version of each application for each individual customer.

Below, we present two experiences in which two well-known cloud services, Twitter and Google Maps, were used as building blocks for developing an application customized to meet the needs of the particular leaning scenario involving a large group with minimum effort, programming only the glue code to integrate these blocks and implement the missing functionalities. The applications have the following characteristics:

- They use cloud computing services from Google Maps to show maps and associate specific data objects to certain geographical locations that relate to ideas proposed by the students.
- They use cloud computing services from Twitter to assess students' participation to rank ideas.
- They use Facebook authentication services to register and keep track of what students contribute to the discussion.
- They implement freehand writing and sketching on the maps.
- They employ time synchronism on objects that are created/modified on the map (sketches, location marks, photos, comments, idea ranking)
- They store the important data on a local server using a XML format.

In this way we also address some of the problems related to control and security inherent in cloud services as mentioned before. This approach has many ideas in common with the one presented in [10], in which cloud services such as Twitter, Facebook, and even SMS and e-mail are used as data input channels for various learning applications. We share one of our main concepts with software engineers:, that cloud services can be integrated into a new application in order to reuse available, well implemented, and scalable functionalities.

References

1. Drummond, A.: Situated Learning and Assessment. Presented at the Teaching and Learning Symposium Wisconsin (2010)
2. Lave, J., and Wenger, E.: Situated learning: Legitimate peripheral participation. Cambridge University Press (1991)
3. Vygotsky, L.: The Development of Academic Concepts in School-Aged Children. In: The Vygotsky reader, Valsiner, V. J. (Ed.), Oxford: Blackwell, 335–370 (1994)
4. Baloian, N., Pino, J. A., Peña, G., and Zurita, G.: Learning with patterns: An effective way to implement computer supported pervasive learning. Computer Supported Cooperative Work in Design (CSCWD), 2010 14th International Conference, 677–682 (2010)
5. Spikol D., and Milrad, M.: Physical activities and playful learning using mobile game. Research and Practice in Technology Enhanced Learning (RPTEL) 3, 275–295 (2008)

6. Silva, M. J., Lopes, J. C., da Silva, P. M., and Marcelino, M. J.: Sensing the schoolyard: Using senses and sensors to assess geo-referenced environmental dimensions. Proceedings of the 1st International Conference and Exhibition on Computing for Geospatial Research & Application, New York, 1–4 (2010)

7. Antunes, P., Ferreira, A., Zurita, G., Baloian, N.: Analyzing the Support for Large Group Collaborations Using Google Maps. Proc. 15th Computer Supported Collaborative Work in Design (CSCWD), Lausanne, Switzerland, 748–755 (2011)

8. Tan, X., Kim, Y.: Cloud Computing for Education: A Case of Using Google Docs in MBA Group Projects. In: Proceedings of 2011 International Conference on Business Computing and Global Informatization (BCGIN), 641–644 (2011)

9. Masud, A. H., Huang, X.: ESaaS: A New Education Software Model in E-learning Systems. Information and Management Engineering Communications in Computer and Information Science 235(1), 468–475 (2011)

10. Jansen, M., Bollen, L., Baloian, N., Hoppe, H. U.: Cloud Services for Learning Scenarios: Widening the Perspectives. In: Proceedings of the 1st International Workshop on Cloud Education Environments, Antigua, Guatemala, November 15–16, 33–37 (2012)

CASE 1

Supporting Engineering Students Learning Wireless Network Planning Using Mobile, Positioning and Web Technologies

---

THE PEDAGOGICAL PROBLEM

- Teaching and learning the principles of wireless communication is a challenging task.

- it is difficult for students to translate the theoretical models that are commonly used in this area into practical knowledge

- Which is the best propagation model to be used ? Why ?

2

SITUATED LEARNING CONDITIONS

- **C1. Authentic context:** reflects the way knowledge is used in real-life
- **C2. Authentic activities:** ill-defined problems
- **C3. Expert performance:** serve the task before it is attempted
- **C4. Multiple roles and perspectives**
- **C5. Collaboration:** collaborative construction and sharing of knowledge
- **C6. Reflection:** enable abstractions to be formed
- **C7. Articulation:** tacit knowledge to be made explicit

5

WIRELESS ANTENNA NETWORK DEVELOPMENT

- Planning
  - locating a set of antennas and simulating the area covered by them according to various models
- Implementation
  - Construction of the antennas
- Evaluation
  - measuring the actual signal strength at strategical points

9

LEARNING ACTIVITY

- Planning
  - planners do the computation for a set of existing antennas according to various models for various sites
- Evaluation
  - Measures go on site and measure the actual signal strength at the sites comparing the actual figure to the simulated ones
  - They have to explain why there is a difference

9

THE LEARNING TOOL

- Coverage analysis tool
  - **Add Transmitter**
  - **Edit a transmitter**
  - **Radiation Pattern**
  - **Evaluate the Spatial coverage**
- Desktop and Mobile interfaces
  - Mobile interface allows students to retrieve the simulated signal strength values at the current location according to all available models while students are working on the field

10

COVERAGE ANALYSIS TOOL

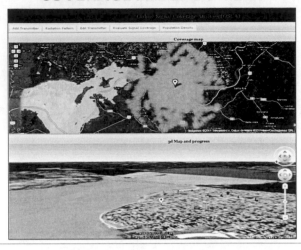

10

COVERAGE ANALYSIS TOOL

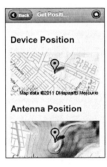

10

COLLABORATION TOOL

- Supports exchange of information and collaboration
- Available for desktop and mobile devices
- Features
  - **Report a Simulation** (available on desktop version only)
  - **Report a Measurement** (on mobile version only)
  - **Vote** (available on desktop and Mobile versions)

13

COLLABORATION TOOL

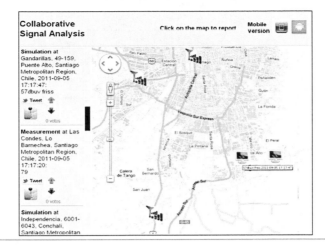

13

EVALUATION

- Were principles of situated learning correctly applied ?
- Does this specific activity introduces an added value to the learning process ?
- The experiment was performed by 28 students, divided in seven groups of four participants each.
- Two of them took the role of planners and two the role of measurers

14

QUESTIONNAIRE

1. *The various developed activities helped me to improve my understanding about how to apply the signal propagation models. - C1 and C2*
2. *The different perspectives both roles provide about the problem being learned helped the group in solving it. - C4.*
3. *The practical activity combined with the theory of signal propagation models helped me to reflect about how to better solve the problem. - C6 and C7.*
4. *The system supported the collaboration among the various members of the team. - C5.*
5. *The collection of relevant data made on the field helps to understand key aspects of the problem being studied. - C1 and C2.*
6. *Observation of the measured data and analysis of simulated data was of great help while solving the proposed task. - C5 and C7.*

14

RESULTS

	1	2	3	4	5	Average
Q1	0	3	6	9	10	3,93
Q2	0	3	14	8	3	3,39
Q3	0	0	6	15	7	4,04
Q4	0	0	4	11	13	4,32
Q5	0	0	0	12	16	4,57
Q6	2	1	3	8	14	4,11

Evaluation results: strong disagree (1), disagree (2), neutral (3), agree (4), and strong agree (5) as an answer. The last collumn shows the average values.

CASE 2

Context, Patterns and Geo-collaboration to Support Situated Learning

MOTIVATION: Learning Patterns and geo-collaboration to support Situated Learning

LEARNING WITH PATTERNS

- Patterns: recurring models which are solutions for recurring problems
- Alexander, Ishikawa & Silverstein (1977): A pattern consists of a set of components: its name, description of the problem it solves, the solution to this problem, an example and the relations it has to other patterns
- Patterns are models for learn, and understand concepts; or solve problems
- It is adopted by many disciplines like architecture, software development, interaction design and pedagogy

Pattern learning Cycle

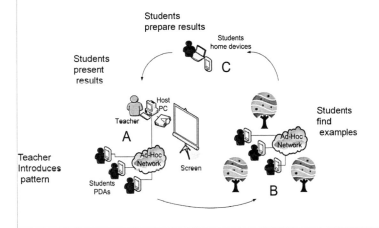

SITUATED LEARNING AND LEARNING WITH PATTERNS

- Lave & Wenger (1988), indicate that learning:
  - is better of when knowledge occurs in an authentic contexts
  - requires social interaction and collaboration - Hung (2002)

- Pattern learning play a significant role in learning
  - to learn => learner discover, register and later apply patterns

- Therefore learning process involves:
  - making meaning by establishing and re-working patterns, relationships, and connections, in a collaborative and authentic context

THE APPLICATION: DEFINING STUDENTS

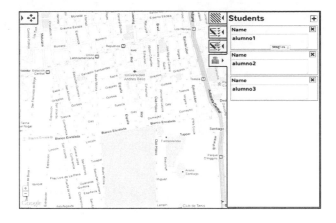

THE APPLICATION: DEFINING PATTERNS (1)

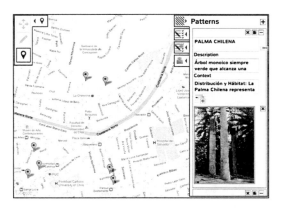

THE APPLICATION: DEFINING PATTERNS (2)

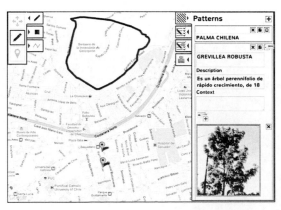

THE APPLICATION: DEFINING PATTERNS (3)

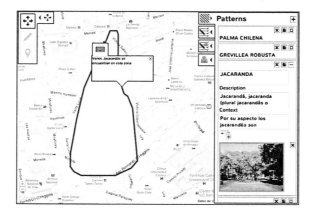

THE APPLICATION: DEFINING TASKS (1)

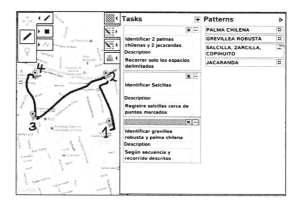

THE APPLICATION: DEFINING TASKS (2)

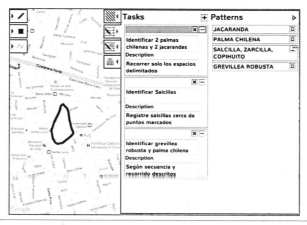

THE APPLICATION: DEFINING TASKS (2)

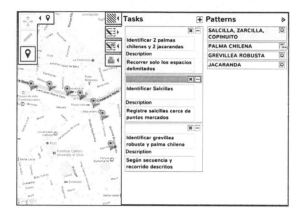

THE APPLICATION: DEFINING STUDENTS ACTIVITIES

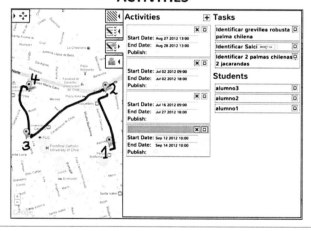

STUDENTS WORKING COLLABORATIVELEY (1)

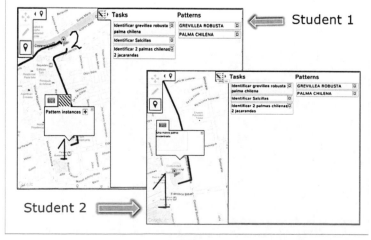

STUDENTS WORKING COLLABORATIVELEY (2)

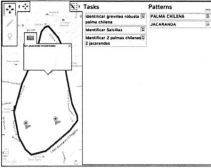

According to the proposed tasks, students follow a path, explore an area, or go to specific places gathering data to collaboratively create instantiations of the pattern when they find elements that correspond to the pattern. In this screenshot three tasks and the one instance found for one of these tasks, instantiations consist of text descriptions, pictures or sketches

IS THIS SITUATED LEARNING ? (1)

- C1. Provides authentic contexts reflecting the way knowledge is used in real life

Patterns instances are searched for in the very place they appear naturally

- C2. Provides authentic activities

Finding pattern instances in natural environments is typical work experts often do

- C3. Provides access to expert performances and the modeling of processes

After completing the field work, back in the classroom the teacher provides examples from the expert's regarding the task

IS THIS SITUATED LEARNING ? (2)

- C4. Provides multiple roles and perspectives

There are two roles: the teacher and the student. In certain cases students might also propose tasks taking the role of the teacher

- C5. Supports collaborative construction of knowledge

Students work collaboratively on the field in order to collect the relevant data and share it

- C6. Promotes reflection to enable abstractions to be formed

Students present their findings in front of the class reflecting about the patterns they found

IS THIS SITUATED LEARNING ? (3)

- C7. Enables tacit knowledge to be made explicit

The system allows students to collect data, relate and communicate them formalizing their unsorted ideas about what they find

- C8. Provides coaching and scaffolding by the teacher

The teacher can help students during the work on the field, as well as back in the classroom

- C9. Provides for authentic assessment of learning within the tasks

Possible patterns and patterns instances are checked by the students and the teacher during the work

A GENERAL ARCHITECTURE

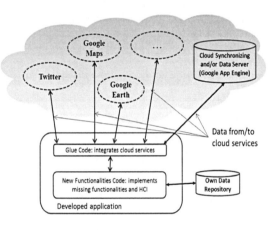

ARCHITECTURE FOR CASE 1

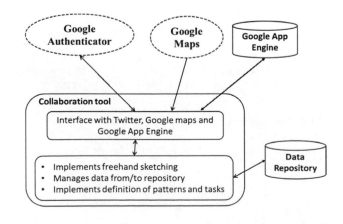

ARCHITECTURE FOR CASE 2

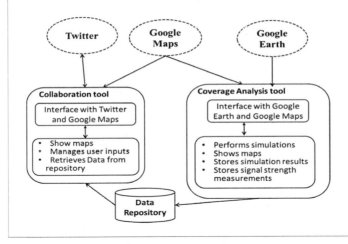

A FRAMEWORK: for developing situated learning applications using cloud services

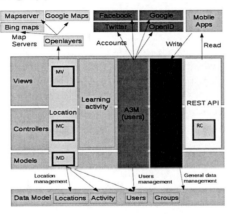

CONCLUSIONS

- Learning activity based on the situated learning theory, with the necessary computer technology to support it
- One step forward, as it envisages a combination of in-classroom theoretical learning sessions with laboratory and on the field work encouraging collaboration and reflection.
- Experiment results show high degrees of agreement with assertions related to these aspects.
- New insights and perspectives related to the design of situated learning activities using mobile, positioning and web technologies.

20

Understanding Collaboration in Healthcare

Valeria Herskovic, Carolina Fuentes, and
Cecilia Saint-Pierre
Pontificia Universidad Católica de Chile Santiago, Chile
vherskov@ing.puc.cl,cjfuentes@uc.cl,csaintpierre@uc.cl

Computer-supported cooperative work (CSCW) is a research area dealing with understanding how groups collaborate while working and how computer systems are constructed and used to support these workers. CSCW has recently expanded to include social computing, studying social behavior and Web-based computer applications, such as Facebook and Twitter, which people use to interact socially. Collaborative processes involve a great deal of human participation. The complexity of human behavior makes it hard to truly understand a collaborative work process and communicate it, thus making system design difficult.

E-health is a research area concerned with systems that support healthcare. This paper presents work regarding collaboration in healthcare in two distinct settings: work done in primary healthcare centers and the work of informal caregivers interacting with patients in palliative care. We explore two different approaches towards dealing with the problem of understudying collaborative work: one based on post-hoc analysis and the other on a more traditional ethnographic approach.

First, we discuss the case of collaboration in public healthcare in Chile. In this scenario, multidisciplinary teams work with families to provide them with healthcare. The team members collaborate by using information from other individuals as the input for their work, talking face to face and asking other professionals' opinions on a patient's treatment. This information may be implicitly stored in information systems, such as the electronic medical record (EMR). We propose a post-hoc analysis of information system logs, using a technique called process mining, to understand a collaborative process after it has occurred.

The second case involves informal caregivers working with patients in palliative care. Here, the caregiver is usually a close family member of the patient. Such caregivers may suffer from isolation and depression, and it may be important for them to be supported, encouraged, and helped by other family members and friends. In such cases, a more traditional HCI approach is used, using interviews and ethnography to understand this social, collaborative process.

Collaboration and CSCW

- Computer
- Supported
- Cooperative
- Work

- … Collaboration, Social Computing, and Work
- … Computer Supported Cooperative Work and Social Computing

[Grudin 2010]

Scenarios of collaboration

- Family caregivers [Fuentes et al. 2013]
- Healthcare [Saint-Pierre et al. 2013]

Topics

- Collaborative processes involve much human participation; difficult to express and communicate
- Modeling languages and visualizations may help understand the collaborative process and design appropriate systems
- First part: healthcare, second part: caregivers

1. Public healthcare: Motivation

Some statistics about Chilean healthcare

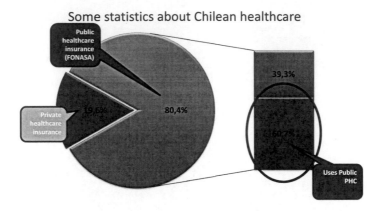

1. Public healthcare: Motivation

More statistics about Chilean healthcare

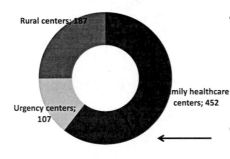

- At least 400 of the Family health centers use the same Information system (Rayen).

- 3 are managed by UC with a different IS.

1. Public healthcare: Motivation

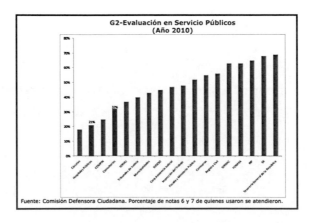

1. Public healthcare: Motivation

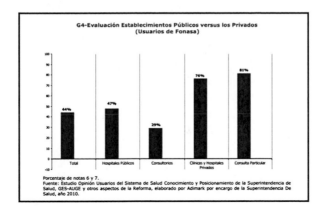

1. Public healthcare: Motivation

	EEUU	RU	Chile (recomendada)	Chile
Tasa Med APS/10.000 habitantes	8	5,8	3	1,9
Diferencia de tasa	6,1	2,9	1,1	
Porcentaje (%)	421,1	305,3	157,9	
Demanda (JCE) Chile según tasa especialistas**	9798	7104	3674	2310
Brecha (JCE) Chile médicos según tasa especialistas.	7488,4	4793,84	1364,4	

Tabla 1. Brecha de médicos APS por cada 10.000 habitantes, según tasa específica por país. *Fuente:* Estimación de brechas de especialistas en medicina familiar para la atención primaria chilena. VI Concurso políticas públicas.

Cerrar X

1. Public healthcare: Background
EMR

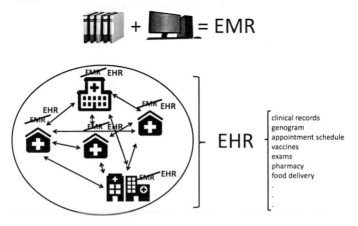

-27-

1. Public healthcare: Background
Processes in healthcare

A process is:

"a structured, measured set of activities designed to produce a specific output for a particular customer... A process is thus a specific ordering of work activities across time and space, with a beginning and an end, and clearly defined inputs and outputs..." (Davenport, 1993)

Then...

- Clinical process v/s Business process (Lenz and Reichert, 2007)
- Particularities (Rebuge and Ferreira, 2012):
  - Dynamism
  - Complexity (patients' unpredictability)
  - Multidisciplinarity

1. Public healthcare: Background
Collaboration in healthcare

- The human being is a very complex animal, and nobody can understand everything...
- So... healthcare professionals have different specialties.
- Due that, we need more than one professional to have a complete attention, diagnosis and treatment.

- Family healthcare in PHC

So, how they collaborate?
- They use the information of other professionals as input of their work.
- They talk (variety of face to face situations).
- They ask for other professional's opinion or treatment, referring the patient.

1. Public healthcare: Background
Process mining and collaborative work

- Working together
- Doing similar tasks
- Standard methodology for diagnosis based in PM (Bozkaya et al. 2009)
- Specific methodology for healthcare process diagnosis (Rebuge and Ferreira, 2012)

1. Public healthcare: The question

Can we find in the process patterns evidence of
collaboration that impacts the results...

...and measure it?

Secondary questions I guess I could answer too:
- Is it possible to identify in every cluster, different characteristics of the
  patients, in order to predict patient outcome and related costs?
- Can we use the results to determine which pattern is better for a specific
  type of patient?
- Could we use this information to improve the clinical protocols, policies or
  treatments?

1. Public healthcare: Related work

- Oncology in a Dutch Hospital [Mans and
  Schonenberg, 2009]
- Radiology department in Portugal [Rebuge
  and Ferreira, 2012]
- ER in Greek Hospital [Delias et al., 2013]

1. Public healthcare: Challenges

- 2012 law

- Data quality

- Particularities of the healthcare
  process

2. Caregivers of patients: Motivation

- Isolation
- Affected social life
- Affected family life
- Health Oversight

60%

Caregivers of patients
have depression.

2. Caregivers of patients: Background

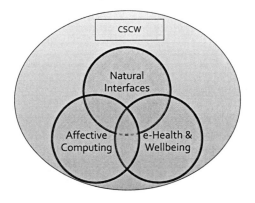

2. Caregivers of patients: Background

- **Related work :** "Caring for Caregivers: Designing for Integrality" [Chen et al., 2013]

  - Qualitative interview study to understand experiencies in caregivers.
  - Factors affecting the collaborative caregiving process.

2. Caregivers of patients: Background

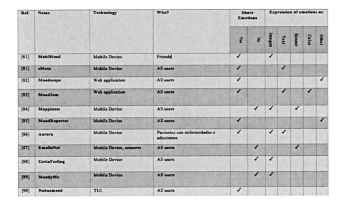

Ref.	Name	Technology	Who?	Share Emotions		Expression of emotions as:				
				Yes	No	Imagen	Text	Sensor	Color	Other
[61]	MobiMood	Mobile Device	Friends	✓		✓				
[81]	eMoto	Mobile Device	All users	✓			✓			
[82]	Moodscope	Web application	All users	✓						✓
[83]	MoodJam	Web application	All users	✓			✓	✓		
[84]	Mappiness	Mobile Device	All users		✓	✓		✓		
[85]	MoodReporter	Mobile Device	All users	✓						✓
[86]	Aurora	Mobile Device	Pacientes con enfermedades o adicciones	✓		✓	✓			
[87]	EmoSoNet	Mobile Device, sensores	All users		✓		✓			
[88]	GottaFeeling	Mobile Device	All users		✓	✓				
[89]	MoodyMe	Mobile Device	All users		✓	✓				
[90]	Nabazmood	TUI	All users	✓						

2. Caregivers of patients: Background

- **Related Work**
- Provide the following key features
- Enable Parent-Clinician Communication & Coordination
- Support Many Data Types, Require Only a Few
- Encourage Consistent Data Capturing Routines
- Provide Glanceable Reports, Opportunities for Reflection

2. Caregivers of patients: Related Work

- Estrellita System [Hirano et al. 2011]
- Aurora [Gay et al. 2011]
- CareNet Display [Consolvo et al. 2004]

2. Caregivers of patients: Problems

- Is it possible to design natural interfaces that capture emotions of a caregiver through self-report ?

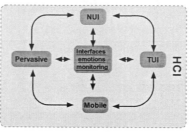

2. Caregivers of patients: Problems

- Is it possible to implement a computer system that supports communication of emotions and collaboration of a family around a patient?

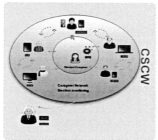

2. Caregivers of patients: Methodology

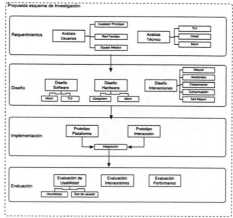

2. Caregivers of patients: Research goals

- Design guidelines to develop system
  - Define key elements
  - Understand communication needs
  - Understand cultural differences (Latin-American vs North-American caregivers and families)

2. Caregivers of patients: Research goals

- A first system prototype: Ohana system

[Fuentes et al. 2013]

2. Caregivers of patients: Research goals

- A first system prototype: Ohana system

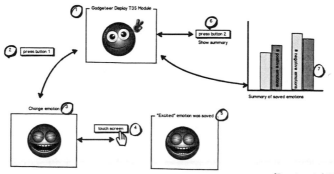

[Fuentes et al. 2013]

3. Conclusions

- Two cases:
  - Public healthcare
    - Multidisciplinary teams
    - Information about collaboration implicitly stored in EMR
    - Proposal: Process mining to understand collaboration
  - Informal caregivers
    - Problems of depression and isolation, require communication, encouragement, support
    - Proposal: Mixed-methods, Interviews, ethnography and data analysis

Business Process Elicitation in a Mobile Collaborative Environment with an Agile Methodology

Nelson Baloian[1], José A. Pino[1], Carlos Reveco[1], Gustavo Zurita[2]

[1] Universidad de Chile, Department of Computer Science, Santiago, Chile
[2] Universidad de Chile, School of Economics and Business, Santiago, Chile

Abstract. Business process modeling is an important activity in organizations that document processes currently being performed. It may also represent the design of a process to be implemented. Process models are used to analyze processes in order to improve, implement, or just document the process for new staff who need to learn how to perform them. The most common situation for analysts to build the model. Nevertheless, end-users are still needed as a source of knowledge concerning the processes. This is known as knowledge externalization. The most common methods of externalizing business process knowledge are interviews and workshops: the analysts meet with the users to extract the knowledge needed to build the process models.

Keywords: BP Elicitation, exploratory study, mobile collaboration, BPMN application.

1 Introduction

Antunes et al. [1] have presented six main challenges for process modeling using technology: 1) automating a fictional problem, 2) the model-reality divide, 3) maintaining model consistency, 4) promoting collective intelligence, 5) lack of flexibility, and 6) missing tacit knowledge. This paper deals with the fifth of these problems, lack of flexibility, which can be explained as the insufficient time required for planning, developing, and deploying highly detailed business processes in the context of agile enterprises.

We assume agile organizations need business process models as quickly as possible. Thus, we report explorations with teams of analysts who create prototype models while they are interviewing users. We also allowed the team members to work in parallel (distributed strategy), interviewing various users at the same time, if they considered that to be convenient. Our purpose was to explore their needs for synchronous communication, convergence meetings, awareness mechanisms, information capture tools, and ultimately, the feasibility of the idea. The teams used MO-BIZ (Mobile Business Processes Capture), a tool we developed that allows Business Process Model and Notation (BPMN) models to be directly built from mobile devices (smartphones and tablets).

2 Requirements

As in software engineering, there are methodologies that guide business process elicitation. Thus, others have proposed agile and lightweight methodologies for this purpose. Agile methodologies are characterized by frequent deliveries, close communication, and reflective improvement. Consequently, our tool was developed to comply with these specific requirements: 1) a mobile interface sufficiently simple and efficient for the initial survey, 2) a mechanism for continuing the work started on mobile devices in a more complete interface on a desktop computer, and 3) ensuring that the work done on both mobile and desktop devices is collaborative, both online—allowing multiple users to work simultaneously on a model—and offline—allowing them to share and distribute the work.

For system user interface, we had the two requirements: 1) portability, so the tool can be used on both desktop and mobile devices with the fewest possible changes; 2) coherence, in that both interfaces—for mobile devices and for desktop computers—have a unified human-computer interaction paradigm while accommodating screen features and pointing devices; 3) intuitiveness, so it can be employed by users without prior knowledge of the tool; 4) flexibility, to allow it to be informally used by people who have no expert knowledge of the BPMN standard for constructing models; 5) simplicity, so it can support a meeting (such as the interviews with the process stakeholders) without interrupting it; and 6) completeness, that is, it allows the construction of models that comply with the BPMN 2.0 specification.

3 The MOBIZ System

With these requirements in mind, the system was developed using HTML5. As a result, it has high portability, no special software installation is required to use it, any modern Web browser will allow its use, and it does not require a special software development kit.

The tool has two interfaces, one for desktop computers and another for mobile devices. At first, it was planned to develop only the one for mobile devices and then export the resulting model to a data format that could be read by existing tools. This plan was discarded because it would make the implementation of synchronous collaborative work among mobile and desktop users very difficult at best. Therefore, our strategy was to first develop the desktop interface without any constraints regarding size or interaction capabilities and to then adapt it to the mobile scenario, fitting the workspace to the reduced screen size and adapting it to the interaction capabilities. The look and feel of the desktop interface was partially based on the one proposed by the BIZAGI process developer [2]. The interaction principle for creating new elements of the model is to start from a contextual popup menu of existing elements; this works very well in both the desktop and the mobile environment.

The first element of the desktop interface that the user sees is the menu bar of artifacts. It consists of a graphic menu containing icons for all artifacts defined by the BPMN 2.0 standard. One of the most interesting features of MOBIZ, partially inherited from BIZAGI, is the use of a context menu when interacting with an artifact on the workspace. We added some additional features to take further advantage of this interaction element. The context menu does not display actions to perform but a list of possible types of artifacts that may follow the current one on the process being constructed. The context menu has two alternative uses. One is to create new devices that will be immediately linked to the original object through a transition arrow. The second is to create transition between two artifacts that have already been created. This is done in the same way as one would create a new artifact, but, instead of dragging and dropping the icon into an empty place in the workspace, the user drags it to the target artifact. Additional features are automatic resizing of the workspace, drag and drop of artifacts, zoom, hotkeys, and double-click artifacts.

The mobile interface is similar to the desktop interface, except in the following ways. The mobile interface is composed of three main parts: the header, the workspace, and the footer. The function of the header is to give the user context information about what is happening on the system. The footer is used to display the Tools menu. The workspace is the part of the screen where the process model is displayed and the user can interact with it. This section uses all available space, except for the header and footer when they are displayed. Navigation in the workspace is gestural.

We also report on our initial testing of the tool, which has shown further advantages of using mobile technology in this scenario. The work described in this paper continues research on business processes modeling presented in the previous Summer Academy.

References

1. Antunes, P., Simoes, D., Carrico, L., Pino, J.A.: An end-user approach to business process modeling. J. of Network and Computer Applications 36(6), 1466–1479 (2013).
2. BIZAGI Process Developer: http://www.bizagi.com/

Business Process Elicitation in a Mobile Collaborative Environment with an Agile Methodology

Nelson Baloian, José A. Pino, Carlos Reveco,
Department of Computer Science, University of Chile
Gustavo Zurita
School of Economics and Business, University of Chile

Continuing work on Process Specification

- Mechanicist vs. Humanistic descriptions
- Descriptions using comics
  - P. Antunes, D. Simoes, L. Carrico, J.A. Pino: "An end-user approach to business process modeling". Journal of Computer and Network Applications, In press, 2013.

Outline

1. Introduction
2. Business Processes Elicitation
3. Agile Elicitation
4. MOBIZ desktop user interface
5. MOBIZ mobile user interface
6. Conclusions

1. Introduction

- Business Process Management (BPM): describe & document business processes to manage their life cycles and analyze them for improvement.
- BPM: efficiency, visibility, agility, risks.
- Model: notation (formal: BPEL, BPMN,...)

Introduction

Antunes et al. (2013) : six challenges for BPM:
1. Automating a fiction
2. Model-reality divide
3. Model consistency problem
4. The collective intelligence problem
5. Lack of flexibility problem
6. Missing tacit knowledge

Focus: problem 5: insufficient time for dealing with processes within agile enterprises

2. BP Elicitation

- Understand activities and identify inputs, outputs, activity flows, decision points, possible parallelism, convergence.

- A major concern: knowledge is spread among people.

- Most common methods: interviews, workshops

BP Elicitation

Problems with interviews:
- Partial knowledge
- Understanding
- Access to information
- Business vocabulary
- Techniques & methodologies

Recommendations: elicitation should be visual, efficient, several techniques, both traditional and collaborative.

3. Agile Elicitation

Agile software development:
- Frequent delivery
- Close communication
- Reflective improvement

Thus, agility for BP elicitation implies:
- Mobile interface allowing construction & editing of field models
- Continue work done on mobile devices on a desktop computer
- Work must be collaborative, both on- & off-line

Agile Elicitation

The interface should be:
- Portable
- Coherent, but using screen features
- Intuitive
- Flexible
- Simple
- Complete: complying with BPMN 2.0

Agile Elicitation

The implementation: HTML5

- Porting with little effort

- No special software is required. Just compatible web browser (IOS Safari & Firefox Mobile for testing)

- It does not require SDKs

4. MOBIZ desktop interface

Development strategy: first desktop and then adapt for mobile scenario

- Look & feel partially based on BIZAGI process developer

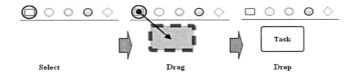

Select   Drag   Drop

MOBIZ desktop interface

- Contextual menu when interacting with an artifact
- Creation of a new artifact: dragging

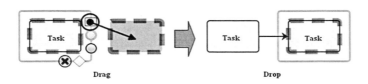

Drag   Drop

MOBIZ desktop interface

- Creation of a transition over already created artifacts
- Dragging as before, but dropping over target artifact. Arrow is created when matching

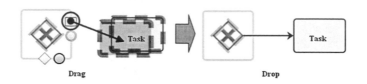

Drag   Drop

MOBIZ desktop interface

Other features:
- Automatic resizing of the workspace
- Drag & drop of artifacts
- Zoom functionality
- Hotkeys: artifact removal, pixel by pixel shifting of artifacts, zoom.
- Double clicks: pop-up window with additional information

5. MOBIZ mobile interface

- Challenge: adaptation should make optimal use of available screen space

- Our approach: all interaction objects external to the model be included in header and footer sections of the page.

- Header and footer can be displayed or hidden

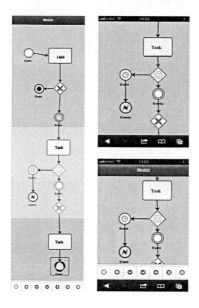

MOBIZ mobile interface

- Header contains context information on what is happening in the system. Additional information may be requested.

- Footer displays the Tools menu. This menu replaces the toolbar and contextual menu of the desktop interface (no mouse to drag items).

- Double click is replaced by a button to edit info.

MOBIZ mobile interface

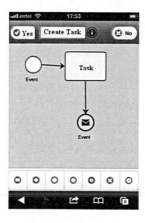

MOBIZ mobile interface

- The body uses all the available space

- Navigation within this section by gestures

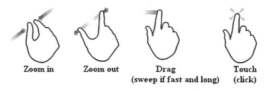

| Zoom in | Zoom out | Drag
(sweep if fast and long) | Touch
(click) |

MOBIZ mobile interface

- Sweep: displacement proportional to speed
- Double-touch: selects and enlarges an artifact
- Double-touch on the background: this gesture alternates between two levels of zoom
- Horizontal sweep with two fingers: navigation through transitions
- Vertical sweep with two fingers: navigation to additional artifacts (used after the horizontal sweep with two fingers)

6. Conclusions

- BP elicitation ‖ software development
- Model can be constructed at the same time process stakeholders are interviewed
- Model is shared among all analysts
- Interviews can be made at the process stakeholders working place
- Reflective improvement to the constructed models can be collaboratively accessed and completed afterwards

Conclusions

- Preliminary tests indicate the tool is usable

- Further work (besides experiments):
    - Is process size relevant?
    - Is team size relevant?
    - Is it possible to develop specific methodologies for BP elicitation?

Using Unconventional Awareness Mechanisms to Support Mobile Work

Álvaro Monares

Department of Computer Science, Universidad de Chile
amonares@dcc.uchile.cl

Advances in ICT technology have allowed people and organizations to support mobile activities with a variety of computing systems. People participating in these activities are typically on the move; thus, their work context changes according to their location. Software applications supporting these persons must deal with these context changes, self-adapting their services and choosing the best way to deliver information to the users.

Providing understandable information to the users, based on their current work context, is mandatory in mobile work scenarios, particularly if they are performing critical activities. Examples include police officers participating in security operations, firefighters responding to emergency situations or nurses and physicians working in hospital emergency rooms. Communicating valuable information in an appropriate way can make a difference in saving lives and protecting property.

An effective information communication scheme requires that the output channel used by the system to deliver a message (e.g., the user interface of the device on which the system is running) must be aligned to the user's input channel intended to receive that message (i.e., his/her senses). Only when both channels are aligned can the information be communicated effectively.

If the channels are not aligned, the system should use some means of capturing the user's attention (CUA) to try to align them. For instance, electronic displays indicating the customer's turn use a beeping sound (i.e., a CUA) to capture customers' attention and thus aligning their input channel (i.e.. their sight) with the display output channel (i.e., the visual message shown on the board). The display's designer assumed users would not have their sight fixed on the display all the time (a very reasonable assumption) and therefore embedded a CUA.

CUAs are in fact awareness mechanisms that provide direct or indirect information to the user about a certain situation. A direct CUA is a signal which not only captures the user's attention, but also delivers him/her the message in a single step. For instance, a smartphone ringtone which is different for each person belonging to a set of people who frequently call the receiver is a direct CUA. On the other hand, if the smartphone uses the same ringtone just to indicate any incoming call, then such a ringtone is an indirect CUA, because the user must establish the phone connection or look at the device screen to discover the caller's identity. The same occurs with the beeping of the electronic display mentioned above. The sound signal indicates that the next person in line can now be served, but the customers must look at the display and read the counter number to see whose turn it is.

In our study, we examined how the use of unconventional awareness mechanisms can help firefighters receive supporting information effectively. The results obtained indicate that odor-based awareness mechanisms can be used to implement indirect CUAs, and probably direct CUAs, as long as the number of signals sent to the users (i.e., message types) does not exceed three. In any case, odor-based awareness can be used as a backup mechanism.

In contrast, vibration-based awareness mechanisms can be used to implement both direct and indirect CUAs. Our results indicate that these mechanisms could be used to improve information delivery, not only to firemen in emergency response situations but also to other mobile workers engaged in similar activities, such as police officers during security operations or paramedics assisting people in medical emergencies.

There are two important steps still to be completed in our research. First of all, we need to determine the average number of vibration signals that can be effectively recognized by an average mobile worker. That will allow us to understand the richness of this information delivery medium. Second, we will use vibration-based awareness to provide supporting information during a real emergency. Thus, we will be able to determine how external variables like surrounding activity and potentially higher levels of stress affect signal recognition. After assessing the impact of these two elements, it will probably be possible to identify the real value of using vibration-based awareness mechanisms in mobile work scenarios.

Unconventional Awareness Mechanisms

Álvaro Monares G.
amonares@dcc.uchile.cl

Awareness mechanisms

- Awareness mechanisms are normally used to deliver context information

Awareness mechanisms

- Use the auditory and visual channel

The senses

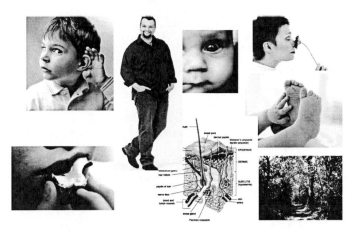

Use of smartphone is not mobile

Awareness mechanisms

- Capturer of the user's attention (CUA)

CUA

- Turn taking electronic display

Capturer of the user's attention

CUA

- Direct CUA is represented by a signal
- Delivers the message

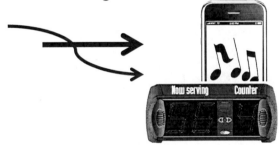

Mobile scenario

- User's attention is not focused on the device

The study

- Odors and vibration-based awareness

Odor-based awareness

- Five different odors – low and medium mobility

Odor-based awareness

- Recognition time (Various mobility)
- Detection and recognition rate

7.2 seconds
100%

79%

Odor-based awareness

- Medium mobilty

4.4 seconds
90%
54%

Odor-based awareness

- Walking person breathes

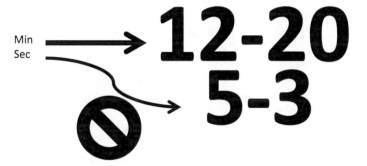

Vibration-based awareness

- Incremental use of patterns tried to identify the number of direct signals which could be effectively recognized by the participants

3-5

Vibration-based awareness

Jogging in a circular path delimited with chairs inside a large room

Detection rate of a tacton

100%

Worst recognition rate while jogging with 5 tactons

84%

4.2 seconds

Vibration-based awareness

- Vibration-based awareness mechanisms can be used to deliver direct information to the user

Future work

- Determine the maximum tactons that a person can recognize
- Provide on a real scenario

Doing Research in Partially Virtual Communities

Francisco Gutiérrez
Department of Computer Science, Universidad de Chile
Av. Blanco Encalada 2120, 3rd Floor, Santiago, Chile
frgutier@dcc.uchile.cl

1 Introduction

In recent years we have witnessed an increasing number of social applications on the Web. In fact, according to Baararjav and Dantu [2], the emergence of this social revolution in 2004 can be comparable to the industrial revolution, where now the accent is on designing and developing software systems that ease social interaction among its users [7].

Social computing is an emerging and highly interdisciplinary research area, linking the study of social behavior with computing systems [17]. Even if its origins are traditionally found in the study of human-computer interaction (HCI) and computer-supported cooperative work (CSCW), today its applications reach far beyond these areas, crossing the buzzword *Big Data* with network science. In fact, the huge amount of available data generated by social applications has facilitated the study of large-scale social phenomena and thus eased the design of new software applications [11].

In this article I will briefly review some of the recent research we have conducted in the Computer Science Department of the University of Chile regarding social computing applications. In particular, in the following sections I will present (1) a framework for helping the design process of software platforms intended to support the activities of partially virtual communities [8] and (2) a prototype application for facilitating computer-mediated social support in older adults [16].

2 Supporting the Activities of Partially Virtual Communities

A partially virtual community (PVC) is a hybrid between a physical and a virtual community. This classification takes into account only the way in which community members interact. Therefore, we assume that members of a physical community perform only face-to-face interactions and that members of a virtual community interact only through supporting systems (e.g., email or a Web application). Clearly, most communities involve physical and virtual interactions in some proportion. The features of a hybrid community will be affected by the features of the physical and virtual communities, based on the degree to which each is represented. For example, a neighborhood community is a PVC that probably more closely resembles a physical community, while a gaming community is a PVC that probably more closely resembles a virtual community.

There is a lack of consensus regarding an appropriate definition of the terms *physical community* and *virtual community* [18]. Therefore, for physical communities, we adhere to the definition given by Ramsey and Beesley, that a *physical community* is a group of people who are bound together because of where they reside, work, visit, or otherwise spend a continuous portion of their time [19]. Regarding online communities, we adhere to the definition of Lee et al., which indicates that they correspond to "a cyberspace supported by computer-based information technology, centered upon communication and interaction of participants to generate member-driven contents, resulting in a relationship being built up" [13]. Based on these definitions, we define a PVC as a group of people who interact around a shared interest or goal using technology-mediated and face-to-face mechanisms. Depending on the community context, different PVCs can involve different degrees of virtualness.

Similar to the structures of physical and virtual communities, the PVC structure is diverse and can be complex. This complexity comes from the fact that these communities can involve social and also (formal or informal) organizational goals. Therefore, the social structure that rises spontaneously through member interaction is influenced by the organizational structure (if this is present), thus generating a hybrid structure that is unique to each PVC community. However, we can assume a hierarchical structure for the PVC since it is the basis of a social group [5]. In fact, whenever a group of people interact within a community, a leader-follower relationship almost always emerges [22]. Therefore, we begin by assuming a leader-follower structure for a PVC, in which it is possible to identify several roles, such as consumers, contributors, lurkers, and veterans [21].

Herskovic et al. [9] state that the requirements of collaboration systems should be layered. Requirements in the upper layers are highly visible to users and developers because they represent services that are exposed to end-users through the application's front-end. Following this line of reasoning, we propose a software architecture composed of three layers (Fig. 1): user, interaction, and community. The *user layer* refers to specific actions to be performed by a single user within the community. Some of the expected tasks to be carried out by a user are logging into the software and managing his/her profile and personal identity. The *interaction layer* refers to all actions and services to be done by two or more users, or with the intention of causing an effect on the community. The *community layer* refers to the global scope of the community, the elements that define the software, and all the principles that directly affect the whole group.

The user layer is composed of five services, one of which is shared with the interaction layer. The registration, log-in, personal profile, and privacy settings manage the identity and visibility of the individual community member. The dashboard is where personal contributions are published alongside those of other members. It allows information to be entered into the feedback loop, where personal and public notifications foster interaction among users.

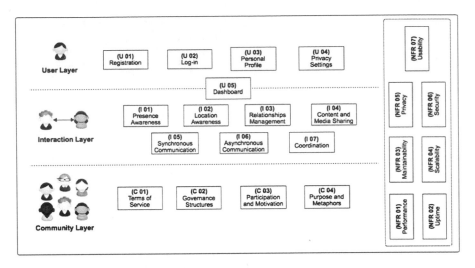

Fig. 1. Software architecture for PVC supporting systems

The interaction layer is composed of seven services: presence awareness, location awareness, relationship management, content and media sharing, synchronous and asynchronous communication, and coordination. The two requirements related to awareness are justified because of users' need to foster face-to-face interactions, as well as requirements linked to services providing different communication channels for users to interact, for example, a message board or a chat room. The relationship management component is a key issue in this architecture. Such a service allows users to identify other members and send an interaction request to them. The coordination service regulates the access to shared resources in the community (e.g., shared object or the communication channel). The content and media sharing component is closely linked to participation in communities that are based on collaborative work. Using such a service, users may interact with each other to contribute or create new content, thus leading the community to evolve.

In the community layer we can identify the four mechanisms (rather than proper software services) that define the context where a community lives and evolves in time. These mechanisms are terms of service, governance structures, participation and motivation strategies, and the purpose and linked metaphors to be used when designing the community. This layer is usually invisible to end-users because its components affect the entire structure of the community. However, it is the layer that has the greatest impact on the design of systems supporting PVCs.

The complexity of the architecture presented in Fig. 1 and the nature of these supporting applications indicates that these systems must be framed in a client-server architecture, where the user layer lives on the client side and the two lower layers are on the server side. This design decision simplifies the service's implementation.

Non-functional requirements (NFRs) are transversal requirements; therefore, they affect all the services provided through the architecture. The proposed architecture considers NFRs and proposes mechanisms to address them. The identification of services and their separation based on whom they concern (i.e., user, interaction, or community) make systems maintainable and extensible. This property comes from structuring the system using layers [3]. We can also expect systems that are implemented using this architecture to perform appropriately because it is a client-server architecture and involves just three layers [15]. Since the two lower layers (which are affected by the number of communities and users to be supported) live on the server, we can ensure the system's scalability by increasing the computing power in the server side. Although system uptime cannot be ensured through this architecture since it does not consider replicated components in the server side [15], it would be interesting to include this feature in the future. However, the proposed architecture partially addresses such an NFR through the use of asynchronous interaction services.

User privacy preferences are stored by the system; therefore, the services provided by the platform must self-configure to adhere to the user privacy settings. Since this information is dual-synchronized (i.e., it is kept on the client and also on the server), it cannot be modified unless the user has simultaneous access to both copies of the information. This information management policy is also used to manage personal and login information. This mechanism contributes to building secure systems. In addition, the architecture requires user authentication. Similar to any other domain-specific software architectures, this proposal addresses the system's usability at the same time as it addresses all the above-listed requirements (both functional and nonfunctional).

3 Facilitating Computer-Mediated Social Support

Today, social media help people enhance and increase their social interactions. Unfortunately, older adults usually lack the required knowledge and technological background needed to participate in these platforms. Therefore, this evolution of social interaction media typically excludes older adults and socially isolates them. For example, according to the 2012 census data for Chile [6], only 28.5% of people over 50 years of age is able to search information on the Web and 25.6% know how to send e-mails, while 70.5% are unable to perform either of these tasks. Moreover, according to Internet World Stats [12], the Internet usage penetration in Chile is 59.2%, the second highest in the region. These values are evidence of a generation gap in terms of technological adoption and usage since adults over 50 years old in Chile account for 28.1% of the country's population.

While seniors prefer social interaction based on telephone, letters, and face-to-face communication, younger generations lean towards mobile computing and social networking services. This has caused the emergence of three different generations, according to their preferred social interaction mechanisms: *digital natives*, who grew up with Internet-based and mobile technology; *digital immigrants*, who positively adopted these technologies; and the *digital illiterate*, who failed in this adoption or were not affected by the introduction of these technologies. If we consider a typical family, it is quite possible that the older adults are digital illiterates, while their grandchildren are digital natives. Figure 2 depicts the evolution of the social interaction channels of a family community during recent years based on the interaction tools preferred by their members.

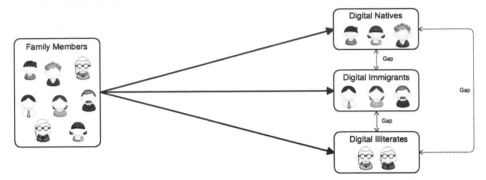

Fig. 2. Social interaction channels evolution

This technological shift pushes older adults to acquire new knowledge. However, elders are limited in addressing that challenge because one of the most common consequences of aging is the impairment of cognitive ability. This translates into a reduction in biological and mental capacities, such as visual and auditory perception, fine motor control, and some aspects of memory and cognition [4, 10]. Therefore, these people need support and guidance to face this complex scenario in a pleasant way [20]. Otherwise, technological adoption by older adults dramatically diminishes.

The social isolation that affects older adults is mostly due to their low capabilities of using technological solutions that were not properly designed for them, such as most social networking services and e-mail applications. This phenomenon leads to harmful effects on their physical and mental health. In fact, social isolation and low stimulation can be linked to changes in hormone production in human beings [1] and, more specifically, to a reduction in the levels of DHEA, a hormone used for slowing or reversing aging, improving thinking skills in older people, and slowing the progress of Alzheimer's disease [14]. This, since social isolation can directly impact their behavior, physical and emotional wellbeing, and interpersonal empathy, it is relevant to identify alternative interaction mechanisms that can be used by older adults.

In hopes of improving mood in older adults and helping them overcome the negative effects of social isolation, we developed a computer-based intermediary system that we call Social Connector. This system is capable of boosting social interaction between older adults and their close relatives. Social Connector plays two roles: (1) to try to reduce the gap between the social interaction scenarios preferred by older adults and by digital natives, digital immigrants, and other digital illiterate and (2) to act as a mood sensor, triggering warnings and other notification mechanisms to alert and support those in need. The system takes advantage of the sensing devices embedded in computers (particularly in tablets) to implement presence awareness mechanisms.

So that elders will understand and feel comfortable with it, the user interface of the Social Connector is simple (Fig. 3a). The available services allow users to perform videoconferences and send/receive private or public messages. A tablet running the system was installed on a wall (Fig.3b) and kept connected at all times to the electrical network and Internet. This avoids elder people having to cope with connection issues.

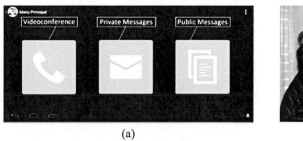 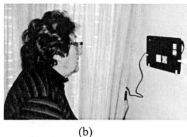

(a) (b)

Fig. 3. Implementation of the Social Connector

The elders use their voice to communicate with other family members; they use their hands only to select the service they require. After a service has been used, the system automatically detects inactivity and presents (by default) the main user interface. This mechanism avoids elders having to deal with the windows used in most software applications.

The videoconference module was implemented using the Skype API. Fig. 4a shows the list of contacts that is visible to the elders. This service allows other family members to call them using the regular Skype system, which typically eases interaction because the communication tool does not represent an obstacle for them. Usually, the rest of the family prefers to use their regular interaction systems (e.g., e-mail, Skype, Facebook) to communicate with other relatives instead of using a proprietary system where they have to log in to interact with the others. This aspect of the system—that is, its usability for adults and young people—was identified as a key design issue during the system evaluation. Therefore, it has been partially addressed in the current version of the Social Connector.

(a) (b) (c)

Fig. 4. User interfaces of the Social Connector

Following the same idea, private messages have been implemented as e-mails, thus allowing family members to use regular email systems to deliver these messages to elders. A filter embedded in the private message component displays only family members' messages on the interface. Fig. 4b shows the user interface in which the elders visualize these messages. Elders respond to private messages simply by speaking (Fig. 4c). A speech-to-text translator converts the voice message and shows it on the screen. If the user okays the message that has been displayed, it is sent as an e-mail. Otherwise, a new message response can be recorded or the user can decide not to respond to the incoming message.

References

1. Arnetz, B., Theorell, T., Levi, L., Kallner, A., Eneroth, P.: An experimental study of social isolation of elderly people: Psychoendocrine and metabolic effects. Psychosomatic Medicine, 45(4), 395–406, 1983
2. Baararjav, E.-A., Dantu, R.: Current and future trends in social media. In: Proceedings of the 2011 IEEE International Conference on Social Computing (SocialCom 2011). Boston MA, United States, 2011
3. Buschmann, F., Meunier, R., Rohnert, H., Sommerlad, P., Stal, M.: Pattern-oriented software architecture: a system of patterns. John Wiley & Sons: Chichester, 1996
4. Carmichael, A.: Style guide for the design of interactive television services for elderly viewers. Independent Television Commission: Winchester, 1999
5. Chase, I.D.: Social process and hierarchy formation in small groups: A comparative perspective. American Sociological Review, 45(6), 905–924, 1980
6. Chile 2012 Preliminary Census Data: http://www.censo.cl (last visit: April 18, 2013)
7. Giles, J.: Making the links. Nature, 488, 448–450, 2012
8. Gutierrez, F., Baloian, N., Ochoa, S.F., Zurita, G.: Designing the software support for partially virtual communities. In: Proceedings of the 18th CRIWG Conference on Collaboration and Technology (CRIWG '12). Raesfeld, Germany, 2012
9. Herskovic, V., Ochoa, S.F., Pino, J.A., Neyem, A.: The iceberg effect: Behind the user interface of mobile collaborative systems. Journal of Universal Computer Science, 17(2), 183–202, 2011
10. Hawthorn, D.: Possible implications of aging for interface designers. Interacting with Computers, 12, 151-156, 2000
11. Kleinberg, J.: The convergence of social and technological networks. Communications of the ACM, 51(11), 66-72, 2008
12. Latin American Internet and Facebook Population Statistics: http://www.internetworldstats.com/stats10.htm (last visit: September 15, 2013)
13. Lee, F.S., Vogel, D., Moez, L.: Virtual community informatics: A review and research agenda. Journal of Information Technology Theory and Application, 5(1), 47–61, 2003
14. MedlinePlus: http://www.nlm.nih.gov/medlineplus/druginfo/natural/331.html (last visit: September 15, 2013)
15. Menascé, D.A., Almeida, V.A.F.: Capacity planning for Web services: Metrics, models and methods. Prentice Hall: Upper Saddle River, 2001
16. Muñoz, D., Gutierrez, F., Ochoa, S.F., Baloian, N.: Enhancing social interaction between older adults and their families. In: Proceedings of the 5th International Work-Conference on Ambient Assisted Living and Active Aging (IWAAL '13). Guanacaste, Costa Rica, 2013
17. Panda, M., El-Bendary, N., Salama, M.A., Hassanien, A.-E., Abraham, A.: Computational social networks: Tools, perspectives, and challenges. Springer-Verlag: London, pp. 3–23, 2012

18. Porter, C.E.: A typology of virtual communities: A multi-disciplinary foundation for future research. Journal of Computer-Mediated Communication, 10(1), 2004

19. Ramsey, D., Beesley, K.B.: 'Perimeteritis' and rural health in Manitoba, Canada: Perspectives from rural healthcare managers. Rural and Remote Health, 7, 850, 2007.

20. Roupa, Z., Nikas, M., Gerasimou, E., Zafeiri, V., Giasyrani, L., Kazitori, E., Sotiropoulou, P.: The use of technology by the elderly. Health Science Journal, 4(2), 118–126, 2010.

21. Tedjamulia, S., Olsen, D., Dean, D., Albrecht, C.: Motivating content contributions to online communities: Toward a more comprehensive theory. In: Proceedings of the 38th Hawaii International Conference on System Sciences. Hawaii, United States, 2005.

22. Van Vugt, M., De Cremer, D.: Leadership in social dilemmas: Social identification effects on collective actions in public goods. Journal of Personality and Social Psychology, 76(4), 587–599, 1999.

DOING RESEARCH IN
PARTIALLY VIRTUAL COMMUNITIES

Francisco Gutiérrez F.

frgutier@dcc.uchile.cl

Online Communities

[Lee et al. 2003]

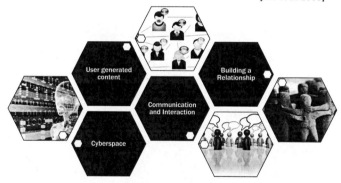

2

Sense of Community

[McMillan and Chavis 1986]

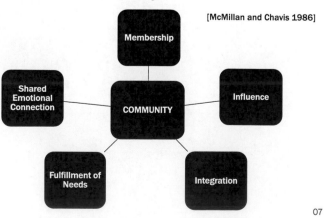

07

Partially Virtual Communities

[Gutierrez et al. 2012]

A Partially Virtual Community is a group of people
who interact around a shared interest or goal using
technology-mediated and face-to-face mechanisms

4

Designing the Software Support

[Gutierrez et al. 2012]

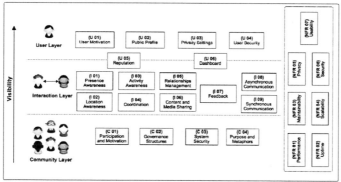

5

Social Relationships and Health

[Cohen 2004]

• Social Support
   • Instrumental
   • Informational
   • Emotional

• Social Integration
   • Participation
   • Sense of Community
   • Identification with One's Social Roles

6

Communication Asymmetry

[Muñoz et al. 2013a]

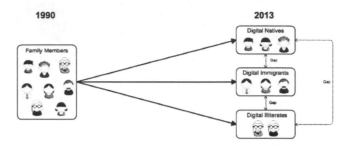

7

Communication Asymmetry

[Muñoz et al. 2013a]

- Understanding older adults and their relatives' availability management, media preference and communication commitment

- Nine semi-structured interviews with adults and older adults

- Understanding communication routines, coordination and media preferences

8

Social Connector

[Muñoz et al. 2013b]

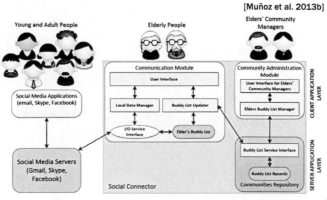

9

Social Connector

[Muñoz et al. 2013b]

10

Social Support: Tracking Emotions

- Identifying the evolution of the emotional patterns of an individual
  - Tracking and analyzing speech
  - Sentiment analysis on text
  - Gathering further information from embedded sensors

- Information fusion: processing these data and inferring mood and its fluctuations
  - Outliers in the emotion distribution

11

References

[Cohen 2004] Cohen, S.: Social Relationships and Health. American Psychologist, 2004.

[Gutierrez et al. 2012] Gutierrez, F., Baloian, N., Ochoa, S.F., Zurita, G.: Designing the Software Support for Partially Virtual Communities. In: Herskovic, V., Hoppe, H.U., Jansen, M., Ziegler, J. (Eds.): Collaboration and Technology. LNCS, vol. 7493, pp. 73-88. Springer, Heidelberg, 2012.

[Lee et al. 2003] Lee, F.S., Vogel, D., Moez, L.: Virtual Community Informatics: A Review and Research Agenda. Journal of Information Technology Theory and Application, 5(1):47–61, 2003.

[McMillan and Chavis 1986] McMillan, D.W., Chavis, D.M.: Sense of Community: A Definition and Theory. Journal of Community Psychology, 14(1):6-23, 1986.

[Muñoz et al. 2013a] Muñoz D., Cornejo, R., Ochoa, S.F., Favela, J., Gutierrez, F., Tentori, M.: Aligning Intergenerational Communication Patterns and Rhythms in the Age of Social Media. Under revision at: 1st Chilean Conference on Human-Computer Interaction (ChileCHI 2013). Temuco, Chile, 2013.

[Muñoz et al. 2013b] Muñoz D., Gutierrez, F. Ochoa, S.F., Baloian, N.: Enhancing Social Interaction between Older Adults and their Families. In: Nugent, C., Coronato, A., Bravo, José (Eds.): Ambient Assisted Living and Active Aging. LNCS, vol. 8277, pp. 47-54. Springer, Heidelberg, 2013.

12

Ambient Intelligence in Metropolitan Regions: A User Interface Perspective

Benjamin Weyers

Virtual Reality Group, Chair of High Performance Computing,
RWTH Aachen University, Seffenter Weg 23, 52074 Aachen, Germany
weyers@vr.rwth-aachen.de

Abstract. This paper investigates the role of user interfaces, examining their implementation and use in ambient intelligence in metropolitan regions. The main focus lies on a solution for modeling and implementing highly adaptable user interfaces in the context of ambient intelligence systems. The paper presents a formal approach for creating user interface models based on a defined set of requirements. Further extensions are described in the final section.

Keywords: user interface, adaptive interaction, formal modeling

1 Role of User Interfaces in Ambient Intelligent Metropolitan Regions

"Ambient Intelligence (AmI) is about sensitive, adaptive electronic environments that respond to the actions of persons and objects and cater for their needs" [1, p. 244]. According to this definition of AmI published by Aarts and Wichert [1], AmI is about responding to people's actions and reacting to them in an adaptive way. Thus, a bidirectional information exchange between *"sensitive, adaptive electronic systems"* and a person is essential for a successful application of AmI in daily life. There are two main artifacts that correspond in order to implement the information exchange between an AmI system and a person: (a) a system for sensory observation of the environment and the person of interest and (b) technical (ubiquitous) installations that actively exchange information with the person. The observation system collects and processes data and information in accordance with the AmI system's purposes (such as those described in [5]), considering a variety of aspects, such as requirements dedicated to the conceived system, algorithmic characteristics, and social constraints, like privacy. The focus in this paper, however, lies on the second artifact, in particular the role of user interfaces (UI) in AmI systems and discusses a possible solution using a formal modeling approach.

Before describing the UI modeling approach, requirements have to be identified by analyzing AmI systems in metropolitan regions (AmIMR) to ascertain the type and necessary flexibility of a user interface. The following list proposes a possible set of requirements for UI development in the above-mentioned context. The list is not intended to be complete, but outlines the main requirements relevant for this paper:

- *Information exchange:* Information exchange is highly relevant for AmI systems and is therefore of great importance in creating UIs in the AmIMR context.
- *Accessibility of services:* One major aspect of AmIMR is to offer access to services and information organized on the Web. Ubiquitous UIs and devices facilitate accessibility.
- *Adaptability and adaptivity:* AmI and ubiquity are essentially based on adaptable and adaptive UI concepts, for instance, if changing the visibility of UIs in dynamic situations or environments becomes necessary.
- *Multi-view and multi-device support:* Multi-view and multi-device interaction is becoming more and more important in a variety of interactive systems. For example, one possible scenario in AmIMR is an interactive combination of publicly available information desks with individual smart hand devices, providing users with access to environment-dependent information.
- *Handling heterogeneous data:* In the AmIMR context, UIs will be confronted with a heterogeneous set of data types and data sets. They must be flexible enough not only to integrate this heterogeneity, but also to interact appropriately with users regarding the data.

Further aspects related to UIs in AmIMR are new challenges in usability and user experience engineering, because the AmIMR context presents different problems than those faced by classic UIs, as can be observed in the context of smart phones or desktop computers.

2 Formal Modeling of User Interfaces

As presented in [9], we developed a formal modeling approach that meets some of the above requirements and can therefore be used in an AmIMR context to create and use UIs. The modeling approach is based on a two-layered architecture. The first layer is the physical representation of the UI, which is directly accessible by the user. The second layer is the interaction logic, which defines the data processing between the physical representation and the system to be controlled. Thus, *interaction logic* mainly describes the processing of events occurring as a result of users interacting with the physical representation and system data being presented to the user. Furthermore, interaction logic defines control structures constraining the dialog between user and system.

Visual modeling of interaction logic is supported by a visual modeling language, called FILL, which is algorithmic transformed to reference nets, a specific type of Petri nets [3]. Reference nets are used for executing a modeled UI by deploying the transformed reference net to Renew, a reference net simulator [4]. Using a graph rewriting approach, as described in [6], the entire interaction logic can be changed and adapted after modeling. This concept can be used to adapt a UI by an expert or by the user. However, it can also be used in a system-side adaptation in the sense of an adaptive UI system. Therefore, formal graph rewriting rules have to be algorithmically generated and applied to the interaction logic using the existing implementation, which is part of UIEditor. UIEditor is a software tool for modeling, running, and reconfiguring formally modeled user interfaces based on the above-described concept.

The whole process of creating and adapting UIs using the approach explained above has been further evaluated through several case studies and scenarios [2, 7, 8]. These studies show that the use of interactive adaptation can be used in learning systems to increase learning motivation, as well as to decrease errors in controlling complex technical systems.

3 Outlook

The UI modeling approach introduced here considers only a subset of the requirements discussed in section 1. The concept of interaction logic makes it possible to model information exchange and offers a high degree of flexibility, adaptability, adaptivity, and accessibility while taking a formal reconfiguration approach into account. Still, multi-view or multi-device scenarios have not yet been considered. Therefore, future work will extend the interaction logic modeling approach to increase modularity of the first monolithic realization and to support multi-view/multi-device interaction on the physical representation level. Further aspects to be investigated include automatic rule generation, interaction analysis and verification, and accessibility issues.

References

1. Aarts, E., Wichert, R.: Ambient intelligence. In: Technology Guide. pp. 244–249. Springer Berlin, Heidelberg (2009)
2. Burkolter, D., Weyers, B., Kluge, A., Luther, W.: Customization of user interfaces to reduce errors and enhance user acceptance. Applied Ergonomics, in press, (2013)
3. Kummer, O.: Referenznetze. Logos, Berlin (2002)
4. Kummer, O., Wienberg, F., Duvigneau, M.: Renew: The reference net workshop. http://renew.de/ (last visit: October 11, 2011)
5. Pinske, D., Weyers, B., Luther, W., Stevens, T.: Metaphorical Design of Feedback Interfaces in Activity-Aware Ambient Assisted-Living Applications. In: Proc. Int. Workshop on Ambient Assisted Living and Home Care (IWAAL 2012). LNCS, vol. 7657, pp. 151–158. Springer Heidelberg (2012)
6. Stückrath, J., Weyers, B.: Lattice-extended Colored Petri Net Rewriting for Adaptable User Interface Models. ECEASST GT-VMT workshop, submitted (2014)
7. Weyers, B. Burkolter, D., Luther, W., Kluge, A.: Formal modeling and reconfiguration of user interfaces for reduction of human error in failure handling of complex systems. Human Computer Interaction 28(10), 646–665 (2012)
8. Weyers, B., Luther, W., Baloian, N.: Interface creation and redesign techniques in collaborative learning scenarios. Future Generation Computer Systems 27(1), 127–138 (2011)
9. Weyers, B.: Reconfiguration of user interface models for monitoring and control of human-computer systems. Dr. Hut, Munich (2012)

Ambient Intelligence in Metropolitan Regions (AIMR)

– A User Interface Perspective –

Benjamin Weyers

Department of Computer Science and Applied Cognitive Sicence
Faculty of Engineernig
University of Duisburg-Essen

August, 29th, 2013

Role of UIs in AIMR

- Information exchange with human users
- Accessibility of services
- Specifies Usability of ambient intelligent services and applications
- Adaptability and Adaptivity
- Multi-View / Multi-Device interfaces
- Possible heterogeneous data

Probably not complete → **Aspect of further research**

Requirements

A modeling and / or implementation approach for UIs in AIMR should comply with following requirements:

- Implement information / data exchange
- Adaptable and adaptive
- Flexible implementation of data processing strategies
- Multi-view and Multi-device interfaces

Possible solution: Formal and executable model of a UI accompanied with a reconfiguration concept

→ **Possible Basis for further work in the network**

Formal modeling approach

1. Use of formal methods for **modeling** and **reconfiguring** of user interfaces
   - Interactive visual modeling
   - Computer-based execution
   - Formal transformation for adaptation
   - (Verification/Validation)

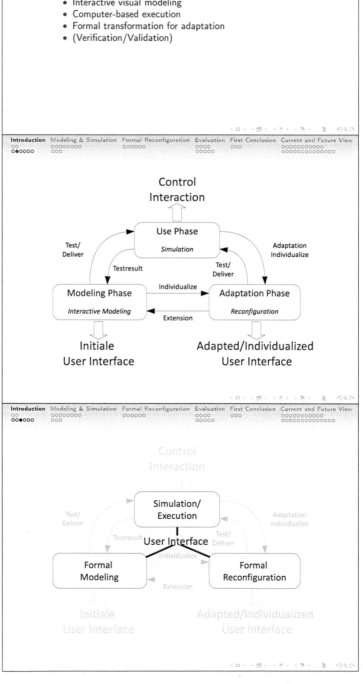

Introduction Modeling & Simulation Formal Reconfiguration Evaluation First Conclusion Current and Future View
oo   ooooooooo   oooooo   oooo   ooo   oooooooooo
ooo●oo   ooo   ooooo   oooooooooooooo

Evaluation

2. **Positive influence** of **reconfiguration** to the interaction of human-computer systems
   - Learning / Training
   - Error reduction

Introduction Modeling & Simulation Formal Reconfiguration Evaluation First Conclusion Current and Future View
oo   ooooooooo   oooooo   oooo   ooo   oooooooooo
ooooo●o   ooo   ooooo   oooooooooooooo

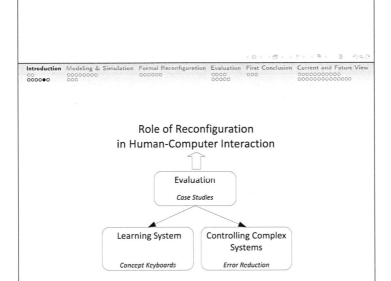

Role of Reconfiguration
in Human-Computer Interaction

Evaluation

Case Studies

Learning System

Concept Keyboards

Controlling Complex
Systems

Error Reduction

Introduction Modeling & Simulation Formal Reconfiguration Evaluation First Conclusion Current and Future View
oo   ooooooooo   oooooo   oooo   ooo   oooooooooo
oooooo●   ooo   ooooo   oooooooooooooo

Overview

1. Formalization of User Interfaces
   1.1 Formal modeling of user interfaces
   1.2 Simulation and Execution of formal user interfaces
2. Formal reconfiguration of user interfaces
3. Evaluation studies
   3.1 Role of reconfiguration in context of cooperative learning systems
   3.2 Error reduction through formal reconfiguration
4. Intermediate result
5. Further steps
6. Final conclusion to AIMR

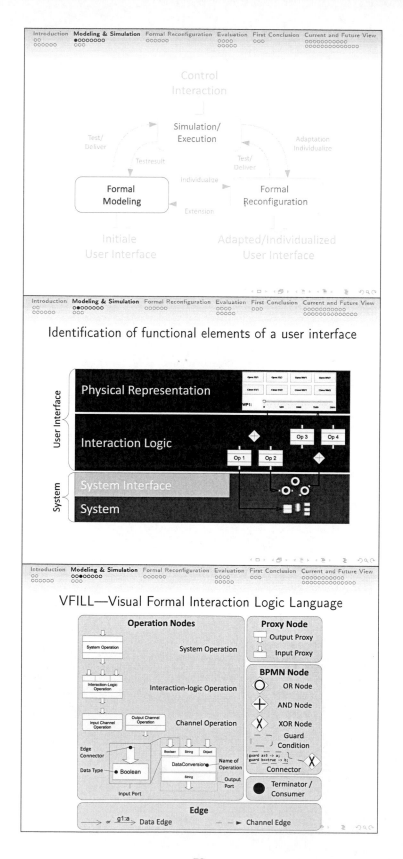

Example – VFILL Model

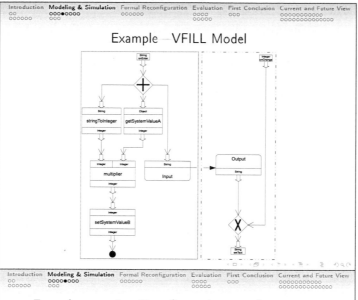

Formal semantics: Transformation to reference nets

Reference nets
Reference nets are higher Petri nets, with...

1. ...an annotation language for representing **typed markings** (**colored nets**)

2. ...an annotation language for **controlling firing of transitions**

3. ...an extension by **references** to let marks reference other nets (or Java-Code).

$\Rightarrow$ Extension of VFILL by **formal semantics**

Example of transformation

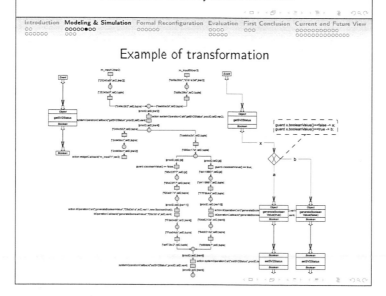

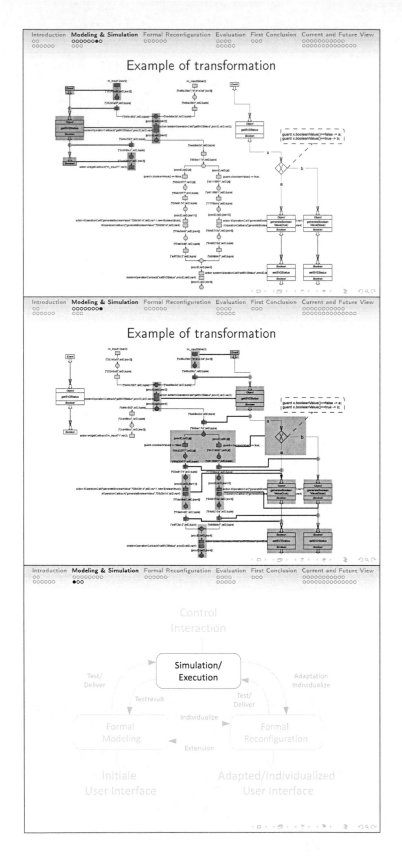

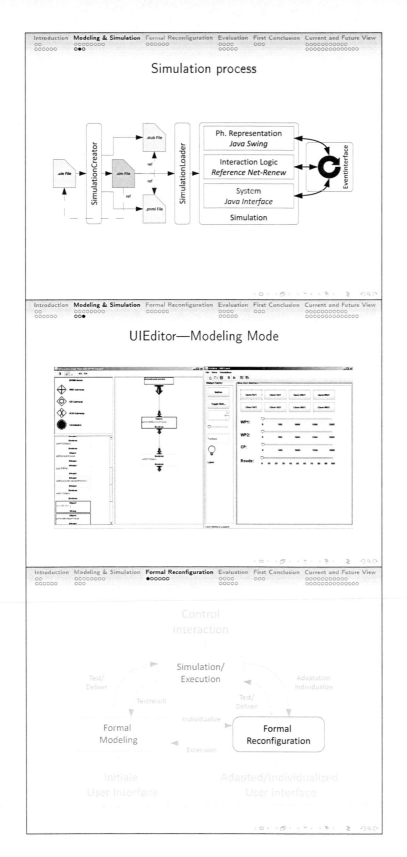

Reconfiguration and Redesign vs. Adaptation

Reconfiguration

Reconfiguration is the application of changes to the interaction logic of a user interface.

Redesign

Redesign is the application of changes to the physical representation of a user interface.

Adaptation = Reconfiguration + Redesign

Formal Reconfiguration—Graphtransformation

Formal reconfiguration
⇒ Changing reference nets
⇒ Reference nets are graphs
⇒ **Graph transformation:**

1. Graph grammars ⇒ NOT well suited
2. Graph rewriting systems ⇒ WELL suited

Graph rewriting system—DPO Approach

1. A lot of work has been done (Ehrig et al., TU Berlin)
2. Simple Handling in contrast to other approaches, such as SPO

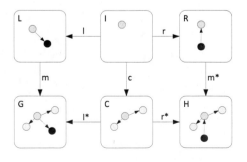

-76-

Graph rewriting systems—Extension to reference nets

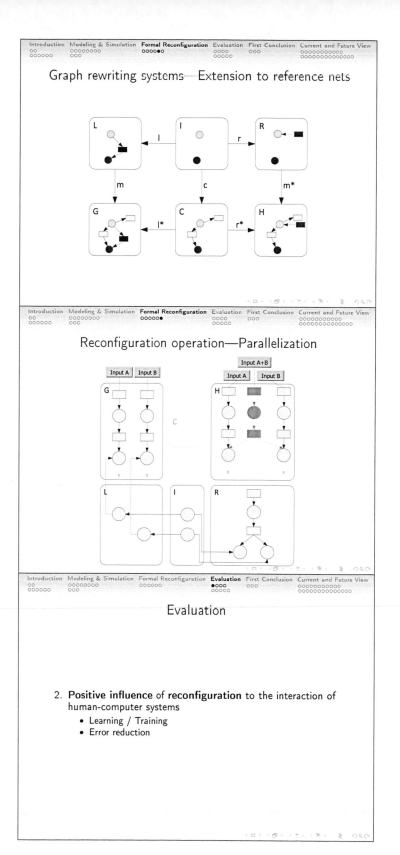

Reconfiguration operation—Parallelization

Evaluation

2. **Positive influence** of **reconfiguration** to the interaction of human-computer systems
   - Learning / Training
   - Error reduction

Role of Reconfiguration
in Human-Computer Interaction

Evaluation

Case Studies

Learning System

Concept Keyboards

Controlling Complex
Systems

Error Reduction

Evaluation study

- Self-assessment concerning pre-knowledge
- Post-Test: Intruder Scenario
- Questionnaire

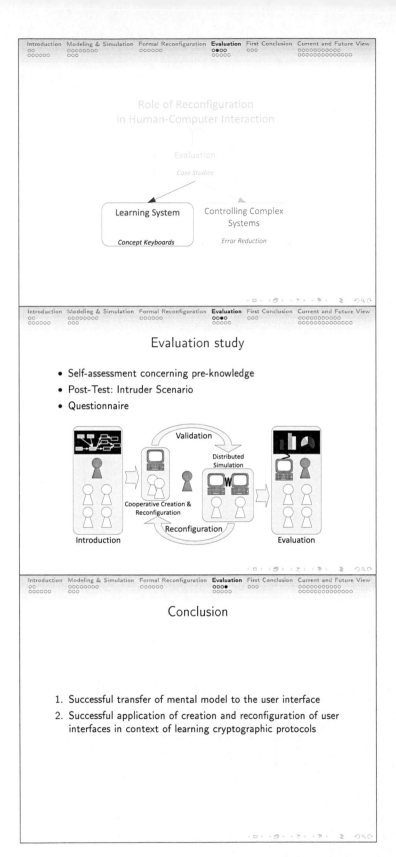

Conclusion

1. Successful transfer of mental model to the user interface
2. Successful application of creation and reconfiguration of user
   interfaces in context of learning cryptographic protocols

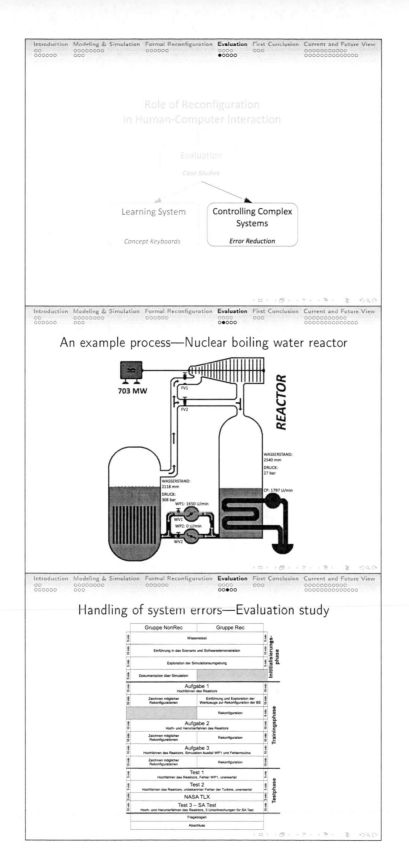

Role of Reconfiguration
in Human-Computer Interaction

Evaluation

Case Studies

Learning System

Controlling Complex
Systems

Concept Keyboards

Error Reduction

An example process—Nuclear boiling water reactor

703 MW

FV1

FV2

REACTOR

WASSERSTAND:
2540 mm

DRUCK:
27 bar

WASSERSTAND:
2118 mm

DRUCK:
308 bar

CP: 1797 U/min

WP1: 1650 U/min

WV1
WP2: 0 U/min

WV2

Handling of system errors—Evaluation study

Gruppe NonRec	Gruppe Rec	
Wissenstest		Initialisierungsphase
Einführung in das Szenario und Softwaredemonstration		
Exploration der Simulationsumgebung		
Dokumentation über Simulation		
Aufgabe 1 Hochfahren des Reaktors		Trainingsphase
Zeichnen möglicher Rekonfigurationen	Einführung und Exploration der Werkzeuge zur Rekonfiguration der BS	
	Rekonfiguration	
Aufgabe 2 Hoch- und Herunterfahren des Reaktors		
Zeichnen möglicher Rekonfigurationen	Rekonfiguration	
Aufgabe 3 Hochfahren des Reaktors, Simulation Ausfall WP1 und Fehlerroutine		
Zeichnen möglicher Rekonfigurationen	Rekonfiguration	
Test 1 Hochfahren des Reaktors, Fehler WP1, unerwartet		Testphase
Test 2 Hochfahren des Reaktors, unbekannter Fehler der Turbine, unerwartet		
NASA TLX		
Test 3 – SA Test Hoch- und Herunterfahren des Reaktors, 3 Unterbrechungen für SA Test		
Fragebogen		
Abschluss		

Evaluation of errors from log data

Sequence Errors (SE)

Expert:	ababa**gh**aaba	ababa**h**aabaa	ababa**h**aabaa	ababa**h**aabaa	ababa**h**aabaa
Test Subject:	ababa**hg**aaba	ab**h**abaaabaa	ababaaab**h**aa	ababa**hh**aaba	ababa**g**aabaa

Swap	Premature	Belated	Repetition	False Operation

Magnitude Errors (ME)

Expert:	ababa**r**aaba	ababa**l**aaba	r – move slider to the right
Test Subject:	ababa**rl**aaba	ababa**lr**aaba	l – move slider to the left

Oversteer	Understeer

Conclusion

Error reduction by individual reconfiguring of user interfaces

---

First Conclusion

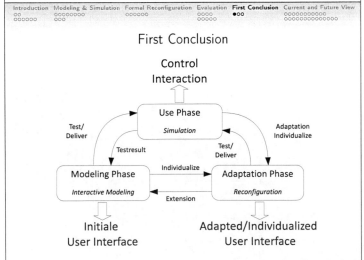

Conclusion

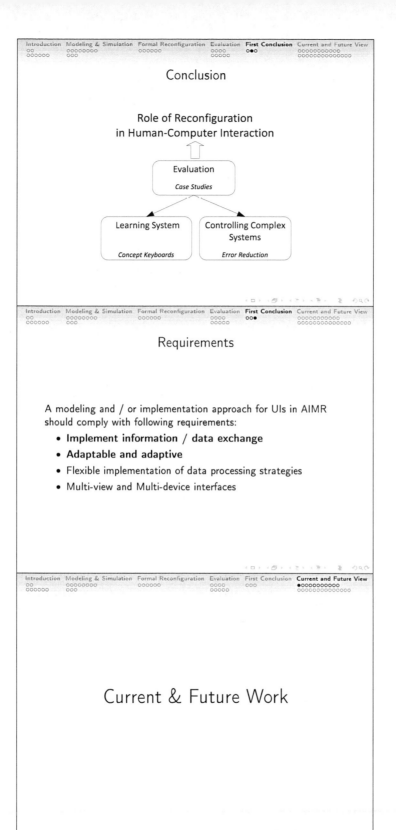

Role of Reconfiguration
in Human-Computer Interaction

Evaluation

Case Studies

Learning System

Concept Keyboards

Controlling Complex
Systems

Error Reduction

Requirements

A modeling and / or implementation approach for UIs in AIMR
should comply with following requirements:

- **Implement information / data exchange**
- **Adaptable and adaptive**
- Flexible implementation of data processing strategies
- Multi-view and Multi-device interfaces

Current & Future Work

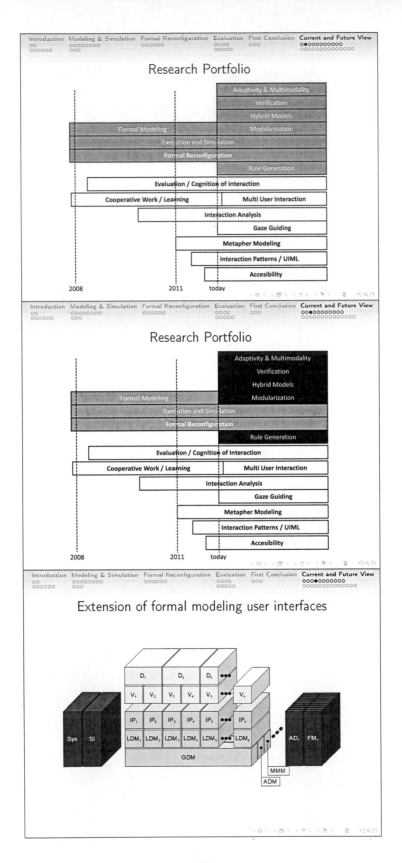

Verification

Work together with Prof. König in Duisburg, on the use of SMT Sovlers for Petri net-based models.

- Which values can be generated?
- What are possible inputs?
- Deadlock testing etc.

Research Portfolio

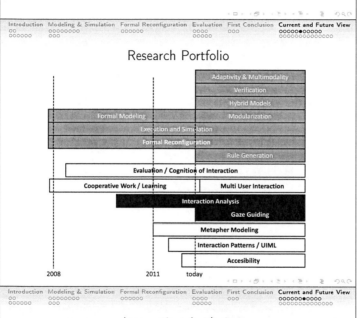

Interaction Analysis

(a) Interaction can be defined as sequence of characters.

(b) Algorithms for parsing character sequences can be used to analyze interaction: pattern identification, uncertain search, etc.

(c) Extending the basic approach to parallel sequences, it is possible to analyze multi-user systems: identification of correlation, patterns, etc. $\rightarrow$ Future work

(d) Formal modeling of interaction logic offers the possibility to introduce analysis into the user interface.

Interaction Analysis

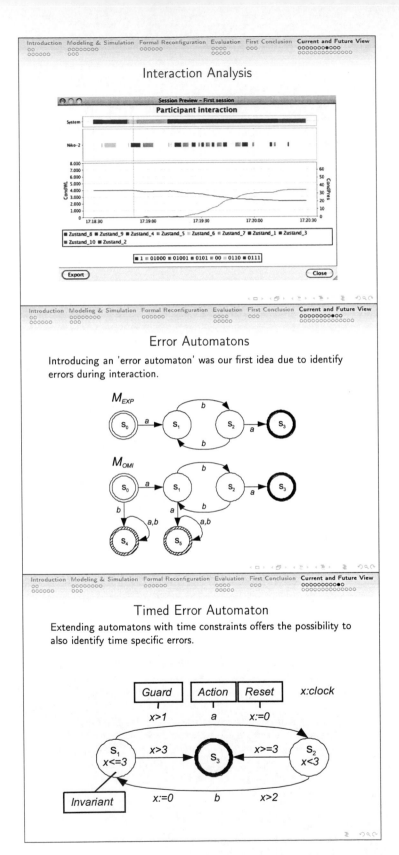

Error Automatons

Introducing an 'error automaton' was our first idea due to identify errors during interaction.

M_{EXP}

M_{OMI}

Timed Error Automaton

Extending automatons with time constraints offers the possibility to also identify time specific errors.

Introduction Modeling & Simulation Formal Reconfiguration Evaluation First Conclusion **Current and Future View**
oo   oooooooo   oooooo   oooo   ooo   ooooooooooo●
oooooo   ooo   ooooo   oooooooooooooooo

Integration into interaction logic

- This aspect is not implemented, yet. Still, Petri nets are (more or less) automatons, such that error automatons can be easily transformed to Petri nets.
- Reference nets are furthermore able to define time-based restrictions.
- It is also planned to introduce 'error identification structures' into interaction logic using formal reconfiguration and algorithmic rule generation. Still, this is future work.

Introduction Modeling & Simulation Formal Reconfiguration Evaluation First Conclusion **Current and Future View**
oo   oooooooo   oooooo   oooo   ooo   ooooooooooo
oooooo   ooo   ooooo   ●oooooooooooooo

Gaze guiding

In a cooperation project with Prof. Kluge, it is planned to use gaze guiding for training.

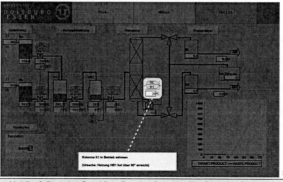

Introduction Modeling & Simulation Formal Reconfiguration Evaluation First Conclusion **Current and Future View**
oo   oooooooo   oooooo   oooo   ooo   ooooooooooo
oooooo   ooo   ooooo   o●oooooooooooo

Research Portfolio

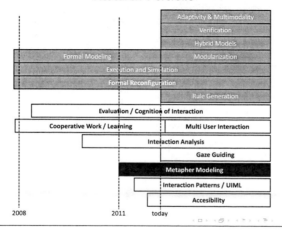

Metaphor Modeling

A metaphor is a simple representation of a complex fact, situation, etc. in a certain context.

Idea: Using (visual) metaphors to represent complex information in a easy to understandable representation.

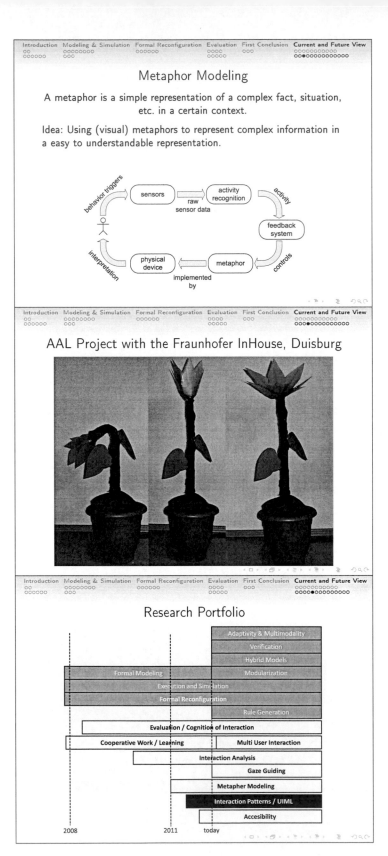

AAL Project with the Fraunhofer InHouse, Duisburg

Research Portfolio

XML-based Metaphor Modeling

Currently we are implementing a metaphor modeling system, wich

- defines a XML-based format for describing metaphors,
- implements a renderer, and
- a simple application scenario.

Research Portfolio

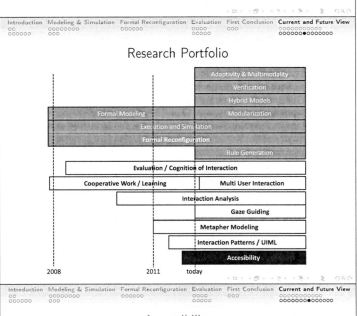

Accessibility

Question 1: Why not implement adaptive user interfaces for blind and visual impaired people?
Question 2: Why not implement haptic representations of complex data for blind and visual impaired people?
The result is one diploma thesis implementing a haptic adaptive interface, and a student research project developing a haptic representation of diagrams.

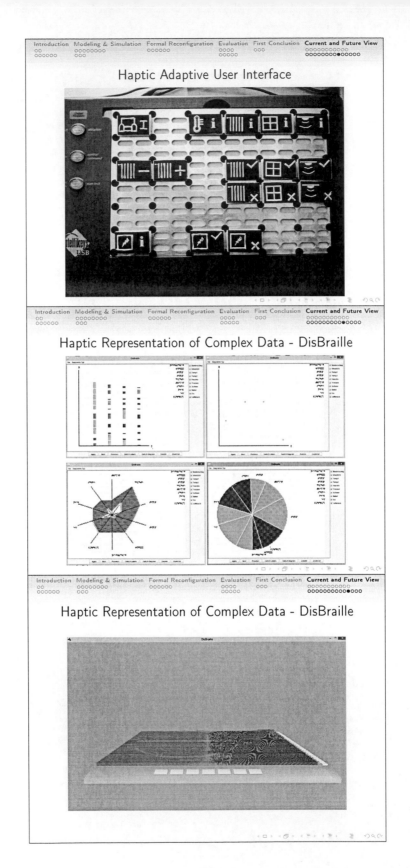

What is coming next?

- Virtual Reality (VR) Group at RWTH University in Aachen, Germany, and Forschungszentrum Jülich
- Cooperation with Lausanne and Madrid
- Work in the Human Brain Project
  - Brain visualization / Scientific visualization of heterogeneous data
  - Multi-View and Multi-Device interfaces
  - Workflow integration

Conclusion

What can I afford?

- Formal modeling of user interfaces
- Reconfiguration of user interface models
- Interaction concepts for impaired, in production environments, in virtual environments
- Virtual environment applications and hardware
- Information and scientific visualization in 2D and 3D

Thank you very much for your attention! Questions?

Towards Critique-Based Context-Aware Recommendation in Metropolitan Regions

Tim Hussein

Department of Computational and Applied Cognitive Sciences
University of Duisburg-Essen, Forsthausweg 2,
47057 Duisburg, Germany,
tim.hussein@uni-due.de, http://interactivesystems.info/hussein

Abstract. This chapter illustrates the potential of interactive, critique-based recommender systems for metropolitan regions. Starting with a brief overview of the field of automated recommenders, it sketches how context - awareness and relevance feedback can be integrated into interactive recommenders for urban regions.

Keywords: Recommenders, Metropolitan Regions, Context, Critiques

1 Recommender Systems

Since the 1990s, recommender systems [16, 39, 25, 26] have been a major focus of research. A recommender system can be defined as a software system which attempts to identify a subset of items that best meet a user's interests and preferences from among all alternatives in a—typically large—information space and which subsequently presents those items to the user in a suitable manner. Recommenders can be found in entirely different areas of application, including e-commerce [28], education [31], news [27], and media libraries such as You Tube [14]. With regard to recommendation generation, many different approaches have been implemented in both industry and academia. These approaches can be roughly divided into content-based [34, 37], collaboration-based [42, 43], and hybrid approaches [8, 23, 24].

Content-based systems incorporate features associated to the objects of interest. User ratings or transactions can be analyzed in order to determine the user's interests or to recommend items similar to those bought in the past or rated as positive. Collaborative filtering systems are based on the purchase data or ratings of other users. Various authors, such as Breese, Heckerman, and Kadie [6]; Sarwar, Karypis, Konstan, and Riedl [41]; Burke [7]; Herlocker, Konstan, Terveen, and Riedl [19]; and van Setten [44], have shown that there is no technique that can generally be considered superior. All approaches have their strengths and weaknesses. Content-based approaches work well as long as decent item descriptions are available, whereas otherwise they fail completely. Collaborative filtering (CF), on the other hand, does not need descriptions at all (which is one reason for its lasting popularity). However, CF has its drawbacks, too: it relies, for instance, on a large user base providing information about their interests or purchases. Many approaches have sought to address these issues, often by combining two or more techniques into so-called *hybrid* recommender systems.

The majority of hybrid recommender systems use CF as the core method in combination with content-based filtering [5, 36, 18]. One popular method of combining recommenders is to implement collaborative and content-based techniques separately and then combine the resulting predictions. Such a combination can be linear [13] or weighted [36]. Alternatively, a collaborative recommender can be enhanced by content-based characteristics, primarily to avoid cold start problems. Balabanovic and Shoham [5] introduce such a system, as do Melville, Mooney, and Nagarajan [33].

The emerging field of social media opens a plethora of possibilities for applying recommender system techniques. Freyne, Berkovsky, Daly, and Geyer [15] recommend items of interest by analyzing the users' actions. Hu and Ester [20] use microblog information to recommend locations to users. Liu, Amin, Yan, and Bhasin [29] augment the content of items that are to be recommended with features inherited from members who have already shown explicit interest in these items. A challenging task is activity or process recommendation—recommending the next activity or step in an ongoing process to a user interacting with the system. With the help of relevance feedback [40], recommender systems learn user preferences through interactive feedback [32].

2 Context-aware Recommenders

Most recommender systems base their results only on the user and his or her interests, independently of the usage context. In many cases, this produces meaningful recommendations. There are, however, situations that can benefit from incorporating contextual information. For instance, a tourist guide that is only based on user preferences might suggest outdoor venues even when it is raining. Examples like this provide the motivation for investigating *context-aware recommendation techniques* [2, 22, 17, 21]. A typical field of application for context-aware recommenders are mobile guides [1, 9]. Additionally, context may be defined by factors that are not directly observable, such as the user's task (although not all authors use the term *context* in this case). Other possible factors include the user's mood, the presence of other people, time of day, season, and upcoming holidays.

Context-aware recommenders have been developed for a wide range of application domains. A pioneering project was *Cyberguide* [1], a mobile guide with location-aware capabilities. Other examples of mobile guides have been presented by Oppermann and Specht [35]; Cheverst, Davies, Mitchell, Friday, and Efstratiou [12]; and Pokraev, Koolwaaij, van Setten, Broens, Costa, Wibbels, Ebben, and Strating [38].

Although the focus of mobile guides was not always on recommending certain things, they can be seen as early milestones on the way to context-aware recommender systems as some systems were intended to recommend possible points of interest in the user's vicinity. Chen and Kotz [10] present a detailed survey of early prototypes developed in the 1990s. Another application domain often used for recommendations is videos, be it in terms of television programs [45, 4], rental services (e.g., the Netflix, http://www.netflixprize.com), or the Internet [14].

3 Critique-based Recommenders

A critique-based recommender [11] is a system in which a user can interact with a recommender by criticizing an initial list of results ("too expensive," "too far away," etc.). This method relies on the assumption that critiquing presented items is often easier for users than forming and expressing their goals up front. In critique-based recommenders, users can explicitly indicate their preferences, for instance, for cheaper products, a different manufacturer, or items of a different color. The *MovieTuner* [46, 47] is a good example of a critique-based recommender. Starting with an initial recommendation, users can interact with the system in a relevance feedback fashion by stating that they like this recommendation in principle but would prefer, for example, a less violent movie with more romantic elements.

4 Critique-based Context-aware Recommendations for Metropolitan Regions

Metropolitan regions provide a plethora of use cases for these kinds of recommendations, for instance destinations for tourists, the hotel and restaurant industry, traffic routing, or nightlife. These recommendations may be generated by combining several input data sources, including social media or (mobile) context information [3] such as the user's location, the current weather, or the current traffic situation. The result could be a conversational recommender [30] with elements of critique-based recommenders, combined in an intelligent, flexible, and extendable manner. This could enable urban mobile users to interactively state their often changing preferences and find interesting venues to explore, more convenient travel routes, or other information.

References

1. Abowd, G.D., Atkeson, C.G., Hong, J., Long, S., Kooper, R., and Pinkerton, M.: Cyberguide: A Mobile Context-Aware Tour Guide. In: Wireless Networks 3.5 (1997), pp. 421–433. ISSN: 1022-0038.

2. Adomavicius, G., Sankaranarayanan, R., Sen, S., and Tuzhilin, A.: Incorporating Contextual Information in Recommender Systems Using a Multidimensional Approach. In: ACM Transactions on Information Systems 23.1 (2005), pp. 103–145. ISSN: 1046-8188.

3. Adomavicius, G., and Tuzhilin, A.: Context-Aware Recommender Systems. In: Recommender Systems Handbook, , Ricci, F., Rokach, L., Shapira, B., and Kantor, P. B. (eds.), Berlin: Springer, 2010, pp. 217–253

4. Ardissono, L., Kobsa, A., and Maybury, M.T., eds.: Personalized Digital Television: Targeting Programs to Individual Viewers. Vol. 6. Human-Computer Interaction. Kluwer, 2004

5. Balabanovic, M.. and Shoham, Y.: Combining Content-Based and Collaborative Recommendation. Communications of the ACM 40 (1997), pp. 66–72

6. Breese, J.S., Heckerman, D., and Myers Kadie, C.: Empirical Analysis of Predictive Algorithms for Collaborative Filtering. UAI '98: Proceedings of the 14th Conference on Uncertainty in Artificial Intelligence. 1998, pp. 43–52

7. Burke, R.: Hybrid Recommender Systems: Survey and Experiments. User Modeling and User-Adapted Interaction 12.4 (2002), pp. 331–370 ISSN: 0924-1868

8. Burke, R.: Hybrid Web Recommender Systems. In: The Adaptive Web. Methods and Strategies of Web Personalization. Ed. by Brusilovsky, P., Kobsa, A., and Nejdl, W. (eds.), Vol. 4321. Lecture Notes in Computer Science. Berlin: Springer, 2007, pp. 377–408

9. Carmagnola, F., Cena, F., Console, L., Cortassa,,O., Gena, C., Goy, A., Torre, I., Toso, A., and Vernero, F.: Tag-based User Modeling for Social Multi-Device Adaptive Guides, User Modeling and User-Adapted Interaction 18.5 (2008), pp. 497–538

10. Chen, G., and Kotz, D.: A Survey of Context-Aware Mobile Computing Research. Tech. rep. Hanover, NH, USA: Dartmouth College, 2000

11. Chen, L., and Pu, P.: Critiquing-based recommenders: Survey and emerging trends. User Modeling and User-Adapted Interaction 22.1–2 (2012), pp. 125–150

12. Cheverst, K., Davies, N., Mitchell, K., Friday, A., and Efstratiou, K.: Developing a Context-Aware Electronic Tourist Guide: Some Issues and Experiences. CHI '00: Proceedings of the 2000 SIGCHI Conference on Human Factors in Computing Systems. ACM, 2000, pp. 17–24

13. Claypool, M., Gokhale, A., Miranda, T., Murnikov, P., Netes, D., and Sartin, M.: Combining Content-Based and Collaborative Filters in an Online Newspaper. Proceedings of ACM SIGIR Workshop on Recommender Systems. ACM, 1999

14. Davidson, J., Liebald, B., Liu, J., Nandy, P., van Vleet, T., Gargi, U., Gupta, S., He, Y., Lambert, M., Livingston, B., and Sampath, D.: The YouTube Video Recommendation System. RecSys '10: Proc. of the 4th ACM Conference on Recommender Systems, New York, NY, USA: ACM, 2010, pp. 293–296

15. Freyne, J., Berkovsky, S., Daly, E.M., and Geyer, W.: Social Networking Feeds: Recommending Items of Interest. RecSys'10: Proc. of the 4th ACM Conference on Recommender Systems, New York, NY, USA: ACM, 2010, pp. 277–280

16. Goldberg, D., Nichols, D., Oki, B.M., and Terry, D.: Using Collaborative Filtering to Weave an Information Tapestry. Communications of the ACM 35.12 (1992), pp. 61–70 ISSN: 0001-0782

17. Haake, J., Hussein, T., Joop, B., Lukosch, S., Veiel, D., and Ziegler, J.: Modeling and Exploiting Context for Adaptive Collaboration. International Journal of Cooperative In-

formation Systems 19.1-2 (2010), pp. 71–120

18. Han, E., and Karypis, G.: Feature-Based Recommendation System, CIKM '05: Proceedings of the 14th ACM International Conference on Information and Knowledge Management, New York, NY, USA: ACM, 2005, pp. 446–452 ISBN: 1-59593-140-6

19. Herlocker, J.L., Konstan, J.A., Terveen, L.G., and Riedl, J.:. Evaluating Collaborative Filtering Recommender Systems, ACM Transactions on Information Systems, 22.1 (2004), pp. 5–53 ISSN: 1046-8188

20. Hu, B., and Ester, M.: Spatial Topic Modeling in Online Social Media for Location Recommendation, RecSys '13: Proceedings of the 7th ACM Conference on Recommender Systems, Pu, P., and Karypis, G. (eds.), New York, NY, USA: ACM, 2013, pp. 25–32

21. Hussein, T., Gaulke, W., Linder, T., and Ziegler, J.: Improving Collaboration by Using Context Views. CAICOLL '10: Proceedings of the 1st Workshop on Context-Adaptive Interaction for Collaborative Work, 2010

22. Hussein, T., Linder, T., Gaulke, W., and Ziegler, J. "Context- Aware Recommendations on Rails." In: *CARS ' 09: Proceedings of the 1st Workshop on Context-Aware Recommender Systems*. New York, NY, USA, 2009.

23. Hussein, T., Gaulke, W., Linder, T., and Ziegler, J.: Hybreed: A Software Framework for Developing Context-Aware Hybrid Recommender Systems, User Modeling and User-Adapted Interaction, 24.1 (2013), pp. 1–54

24. Hussein, T., Linder, T., and Ziegler, J.: A Context-Aware Shopping Portal Based on Semantic Models, Semantic Models for Adaptive Interactive Systems, Hussein, T., Paulheim, H., Lukosch, S., Ziegler, J., and Calvary, G. (eds.), Human-Computer Interaction. Springer, 2013

25. Jannach, D., Zanker, M., Felfernig, A., and Friedrich, G.: Recommender Systems: An Introduction, Cambridge University Press, 2010

26. Kaindl, H., Wach, E.P., Okoli, A., Popp, R., Hoch, R., Gaulke, W., and Hussein, T.: Semi-Automatic Generation of Recommendation Processes and Their GUIs, IUI '13: Proceedings of the18th International Conference on Intelligent User Interfaces, 2013

27. Li, L., Chu, W., Langford, J., and Schapire, R.E.: A Contextual-Bandit Approach to Personalized News Article Recommendation, WWW '10: Proceedings of the 19th International Conference on World Wide Web, 2010

28. Linden, G., Smith, B., and York, J.: Amazon.com Recommendations: Item-to-Item Collaborative Filtering, IEEE Internet Computing 7.1 (2003), pp. 76–80

29. Liu, H., Amin, M., Yan, B., and Bhasin, A.: Generating Supplemental Content Information Using Virtual Profiles, Rec- Sys '13: Proceedings of the 7th ACM Conference on Recommender Systems, New York, NY, USA: ACM, 2013, pp. 295–302

30. Mahmood, T., and Ricci, F.: Improving recommender systems with adaptive conversational strategies. HT '09: Proceedings of the20th ACM conference on Hypertext and Hypermedia, ACM, 2009, pp. 73–82

31. Manouselis, N., Drachsler, H., Vuorikari, R., Hummel, H., and Koper, R.: Recommender Systems in Technology Enhanced Learning, Recommender Systems Handbook, Ricci, F., Rokach, L., Shapira, B., and Kantor, P. B. (eds.), Berlin: Springer, 2010, pp. 387–415

32. Mei, T., Yang, B., Hua, X., and Li, S.: Contextual Video Recommendation by Multimodal Relevance and User Feedback, ACM Transactions on Information Systems 29.2 (2011), pp. 1–24

33. Melville, P., Mooney, R.J., and Nagarajan, R.: Content-Boosted Collaborative Filtering for Improved Recommendations, Proceedings of the 18th National Conference on Artificial Intelligence, Menlo Park, CA, USA: AAAI Press, 2002, pp. 187–192

34. Mooney, R.J., and Roy, L.: Content-Based Book Recommending Using Learning for Text Categorization, Proceedings of the 5th ACM Conference on Digital Libraries, New

York, NY, USA: ACM, 2000, pp. 195–204 ISBN: 1-58113-231-X

35. Oppermann, R., and Specht, M.: A Nomadic Information System for Adaptive Exhibition Guidance, Archives & Museum Informatics, 13.2 (1999), pp. 127–138

36. Pazzani, M.J.: A Framework for Collaborative, Content-Based and Demographic Filtering, Artificial Intelligence Review, 13.5-6 (1999), pp. 393–408 ISSN: 0269-2821

37. Pazzani, M.J., and Billsus, D., Content-Based Recommendation Systems, The Adaptive Web. Methods and Strategies of Web Personalization, Brusilovsky, P., Kobsa, A., and Nejdl, W. (eds.), Lecture Notes in Computer Science, Vol. 4321, Berlin: Springer, 2007, pp. 325–341

38. Pokraev, S., Koolwaaij, J., van Setten, M., Broens, T., Dockhorn Costa, P., Wibbels, M., Ebben, P., and Strating, P.: Service Platform for Rapid Development and Deployment of Context-Aware, Mobile Applications, ICWS '05: Proceedings of the 2005 IEEE International Conference on Web Services, Washington, DC, USA: IEEE Computer Society, 2005, pp. 639–646 ISBN: 0-7695-2409-5

39. Resnick, P., and Varian, H.R.: Recommender Systems, Communications of the ACM, 40.3 (1997), pp. 56–58 ISSN: 0001-0782

40. Salton, G., and Buckley, C.: Improving Retrieval Performance by Relevance Feedback,, Readings in Information Retrieval, Morgan Kaufmann, 1997, pp. 355–364

41. Sarwar, B., Karypis, G., Konstan, J.A., and Riedl, J.: Analysis of Recommendation Algorithms for E-Commerce, EC '00: Proceedings of the 2nd ACM Conference on Electronic Commerce, New York, NY, USA: ACM, 2000, pp. 158–167 ISBN: 1-58113-272-7

42. Sarwar, B., Karypis, G., Konstan, J.A., and Riedl, J.: Item-based Collaborative Filtering Recommendation Algorithms, WWW'11: Proceedings of the 10th International Conference on World Wide Web, Shen, V. Y., Saito, N., Lyu, M. R., and Zurko, M. E. (eds.), Hong Kong: ACM, 2001, pp. 285–295 ISBN: 1-58113-348-0

43. Schafer, J.B., Frankowski, D., Herlocker, J.L., and Sen, S.: Collaborative Filtering Recommender Systems, The Adaptive Web. Methods and Strategies of Web Personalization, Brusilovsky, P., Kobsa, A., and Nejdl, W. (eds.), Lecture Notes in Computer Science, Vol. 4321, Berlin: Springer, 2007, pp. 291–324

44. van Setten, M.: Supporting People in Finding Information: Hybrid Recommender Systems and Goal-Based Structuring, Doctoral dissertation, University of Twente, The Netherlands, 2005

45. van Setten, M., Veenstra, M., Nijholt, A., and van Dijk, B.: Prediction Strategies in a TV Recommender System: Framework and Experiments, Proceedings IADIS International WWW/Internet Conference 2003, pp. 203–210

46. Vig, J., Sen, S., and Riedl, J.: Navigating the tag genome, IUI '11: Proceedings of the 16th International Conference on Intelligent User Interfaces, New York, NY, USA: ACM, 2011, pp. 93–102

47. Vig, J., Sen, S., and Riedl, J.: The Tag Genome: Encoding Community Knowledge to Support Novel Interaction, ACM Transactions on Interactive Intelligent Systems, 2.3 (2012), 13:1–13:44

Context-aware Positioning Model to Support Ubiquitous Applications

Daniel Moreno Córdova, Sergio F. Ochoa
University of Chile, Santiago, Chile
{dmoreno, sochoa}@dcc.uchile.cl

Abstract. This thesis proposal addresses the challenge of ubiquitous positioning of mobile devices in heterogeneous scenarios. Most mobile devices can access positioning services only under certain circumstances or in specific scenarios, such as outdoors for GPS. We believe that these devices could attempt to sense their current scenario (context) to determine the best positioning strategy available or to ask their peers to relay their positions if possible. This would potentially enable all participants in a highly mobile ad-hoc network to determine their positions with varying degrees of accuracy, even if they cannot access a scenario's positioning services directly.

Keywords: positioning, location awareness, ubiquitous computing, context awareness, low energy cost

1 Introduction

Mobile devices, particularly slates and smartphones, have become increasingly popular in recent years, thanks to the advances in wireless communications and computing capabilities. One of their key characteristics is their portability, which allows users to carry and use these devices almost anywhere with minimal effort. This has opened several opportunities to develop software solutions that provide services depending on the user's location, for instance, information delivery to visitors inside a museum or to passersby when they are in a certain area. Moreover, these devices are embedding more and more sensing capabilities that allow users to capture on-demand information about their surrounding physical environment, thus opening various opportunities to perform ubiquitous computing.

This new computing scenario presents a number of challenges to developers, such as providing context-aware services. When a user moves from one place to another, his/her current work context usually varies; therefore, ubiquitous applications must be able to detect these changes and self-adapt accordingly. Although the user's context has more than one dimension, the specific focus of this thesis is on determining the position of the resources participating in a ubiquitous computing scenario. Such resources include the users of ubiquitous applications, autonomous devices, and points of interest in the computing environment. Determining the position of these resources is necessary in order to provide location awareness to the users. This awareness category is a key design aspect in most ubiquitous applications and is strongly dependent on the devices' capabilities to sense the environment.

Most solutions that allow resource positioning address either only indoor or only outdoor positioning, which is not particularly appropriate to support ubiquitous applications, as mobile users do not discriminate between indoor and outdoor scenarios during their activities. To overcome this issue, some hybrid proposals provide indoor and outdoor positioning services. However, these proposals are network intensive (i.e., energy demanding), which jeopardizes the use of these solutions in ubiquitous systems that run on mobile units, because the energy autonomy of these devices is usually low. Moreover, most proposals for hybrid positioning do not address the heterogeneity of devices and physical environments that are usually present in ubiquitous computing scenarios. Although using a combination of indoor and outdoor positioning methods could provide a degree of ubiquitous positioning, the challenge of minimizing the energy consumption involved in the positioning process still needs to be addressed.

2 Positioning

Positioning techniques can be roughly divided into two categories based on the scenarios in which they work best: indoor and outdoor [1]. It is widely believed that outdoor positioning has already been solved by geographical positioning systems (GPS) [2]. However, indoor positioning remains an open research area, in which several approaches have been proposed that attempt to address this challenge [3, 4, 5]. Most positioning systems measure and process one or more signals available in the physical scenario in order to estimate the position of a resource. These systems use different kinds of technologies (e.g., infrared and radio frequency) and positioning techniques [6]. In order to meet the users' needs and offer adaptive ubiquitous services, a positioning system must allow on-demand location of resources in almost any physical environment.

Depending on the type of data that is used and how the position estimation is performed, positioning techniques can be classified in four categories [3]: triangulation, proximity, fingerprinting, and vision analysis. Triangulation techniques use the properties of triangles to determine the position of a target resource [6, 7, 8, 9]. Proximity-based techniques assign the closest base station's position to a target resource [2, 10, 11, 12]. Fingerprinting techniques use signal measurements to elaborate a positioning grid and assign the target resources a position within the grid based on their own readings [3, 13, 14]. Vision analysis techniques make use of image or video capture (typically using computer vision) to determine the position of resources in a physical scenario [2, 15, 16, 17].

3 Our Proposal

This thesis proposal hypothesizes that sensing and sharing particular context information about the work environment and the participating devices could help address this challenge. In particular, the thesis proposes to define a context-aware indoor-outdoor positioning model that enables regular positioning (i.e., positioning resources with an error range of up to seven meters) involving low energy consumption.

The model is intended to provide a smooth transition among currently available positioning services in indoor and outdoor scenarios, allowing ubiquitous applications to consume the positioning services of the model in a transparent manner, regardless of the physical scenario and the participating devices. The challenge of providing indoor and outdoor positioning in a smooth and transparent way is still an open problem in ubiquitous computing. In order to address this challenge, mobile devices could sense the environment and utilize the contextual information not only to determine which positioning strategies can be used in each scenario, but also which ones would allow them to consume less energy; that is, it would enable them to perform a green context-aware positioning.

The model proposed in this thesis will be developed using an iterative methodology based on case studies. Initially, simulations will be performed in order to develop a positioning strategy, which will yield results that will help us formalize the model. Then, additional simulations and evaluations in real scenarios will be conducted. These results will allow us to determine the level of validity of the stated hypotheses. The location awareness services provided by the model will be implemented in a software framework, and they will be available through an application programming interface (API). Developers of ubiquitous applications can access and utilize these services, thus reducing the risks and effort of developing this type of system. In this way, the positioning process would be transparent to the user, the device sensing the heterogeneity of its physical scenario and participating devices and determining the most appropriate positioning method available.

Since the model will attempt to maximize the positioning capabilities of the participating devices while minimizing energy consumption during the process, this proposal would show remarkable usefulness and usability in ubiquitous computing environments. Furthermore, it can be used to support various applications, such as monitoring the elderly, supporting navigation by the visually impaired, providing geo-localized information to tourists, and supporting firefighters during urban search and rescue activities.

4 Our Goals

The general goal of this thesis is to propose a context-aware positioning model able to perform regular positioning of resources in indoor and outdoor scenarios in a transparent manner. The model will consider the heterogeneity of devices that usually participate in ubiquitous computing solutions. It will be compared to the proposals of Liu et. al. [18] and Dai et al. [19] (the most suitable models supporting collaborative positioning and energy saving in indoor and outdoor scenarios, respectively). As a result, it is expected that the proposed model will extend the positioning capability of the participating devices, maintaining low energy consumption during the process.

So far, our goals are to:

- identify and characterize the context variables from both the physical environment (e.g., network availability) and the participating devices (e.g., their sensing and positioning capabilities) required to identify the user's work and location context.
- define a strategy for managing the context information that will allow the positioning model to increase the chances of performing resource positioning while minimizing energy consumption.
- define and formalize the context-aware positioning method.
- define and implement a set of location awareness services that can be reused by developers of ubiquitous applications.

References

1. Hofmann-Wellenhof, B., Lichtenegger, H., and Collins, J.: Global positioning system: Theory and practice. Springer Press, Wien, Austria (1993)
2. Gu, Y., Lo, A., and Niemegeers, I.: A survey of indoor positioning systems for wireless personal networks. IEEE Communications Surveys & Tutorials 11(1), 13–32 (2009)
3. Liu, H., Darabi, H., Banerjee, P. and Liu, J.: Survey of wireless indoor positioning techniques and systems. IEEE Transactions on Systems, Man, and Cybernetics, Part C: Applications and Reviews 37(6), 1067–1080 (2007)
4. Ruiz-López, T., Garrido, J., Benghazi, K. and Chung, L.: A survey on indoor positioning systems: Foreseeing a quality design. Distributed Computing and Artificial Intelligence, 373–380 (2010)
5. Chen, G. and Kotz, D.: A survey of context-aware mobile computing research. Technical Report TR2000-381, Vol. 1, No. 2.1, Department of Computer Science, Dartmouth College (2000)
6. Hightower, J. and Borriello, G.: Location systems for ubiquitous computing. IEEE Computer 34(8), 57–66 (2001)
7. Vera, R., Ochoa, S.F. and Aldunate, R.G.: EDIPS: An Easy to Deploy Indoor Positioning System to support loosely coupled mobile work. Personal and Ubiquitous Computing 15(4), 365–376 (2011)
8. Chen, J.C., Wang, Y.C., Maa, C.S. and Chen, J.T.: Network-side mobile position location using factor graphs. IEEE Transactions on Wireless Communications 5(10), 2696–2704 (2006)
9. Günther, A. and Hoene, C.: Measuring round trip times to determine the distance between WLAN nodes. Proceedings of the 4th IFIP-TC6 international conference on Networking Technologies, Services, and Protocols, Performance of Computer and Communication Networks, Mobile and Wireless Communication Systems, Waterloo, Canada, 768–779 (2005)
10. Bravo, J., Hervás, R., Sánchez, I., Chavira, G. and Nava, S.: Visualization services in a conference context: An approach by RFID technology. Journal of Universal Computer Science 12(3), 270–283 (2006)
11. Trevisani, E. and Vitaletti, A.: Cell-ID location technique, limits and benefits: An experimental study. IEEE 6th Workshop on Mobile Computing Systems and Applications (WMCSA'04), 51–60 (2004)
12. Chon, H.D., Jun, S., Jung, H. and An, S.W.: Using RFID for accurate positioning. Journal of Global Positioning Systems 3 (1 & 2), 32–39 (2004)

13. Wassi, G.I., Despins, C., Grenier, D. and Nerguizian, C.: Indoor location using received signal strength of IEEE 802.11 b access point. IEEE Canadian Conference on Electrical and Computer Engineering, 1367–1370 (2005)
14. Kontkanen, P., Myllymaki, P., Roos, T., Tirri, H., Valtonen, K. and Wettig, H.: Topics in probabilistic location estimation in wireless networks. IEEE 15th International Symposium on Personal, Indoor and Mobile Radio Communications (PIMRC'04) 2, 1052–1056 (2004)
15. Brumitt, B., Meyers, B., Krumm, J., Kern, A. and Shafer, S.: Easyliving: Technologies for intelligent environments. Handheld and ubiquitous computing, Springer Press, 97–119 (2000)
16. Maybeck, P.S.: The Kalman filter: An introduction to concepts. Autonomous Robot Vehicles, Springer Press, 194–204 (1990)
17. Thrun, S.: Simultaneous localization and mapping. Robotics and cognitive approaches to spatial mapping, 13–41 (2008)
18. Liu, H., Gan, Y., Yang, J., Sidhom, S., Wang, Y., Chen, Y. and Ye, F.: Push the limit of WiFi based localization for smartphones. Proceedings of the 18th ACM Annual International Conference on Mobile Computing and Networking (MobiCom'12), New York, USA, 305–316 (2012)
19. Dai, M., Sottile, F., Spirito, M.A., and Garello, R.: An Energy Efficient Tracking algorithm in UWB-based sensor networks. IEEE 8th International Conference on Wireless and Mobile Computing, Networking and Communications (WiMob'12), 173–178 (2012)

Context-aware Positioning Model to Support Ubiquitous Applications

Daniel Moreno

SADUE'13 Workshop
August 30th, Santiago de Chile

Daniel Moreno, SADUE'13   1

Roadmap

- Motivation
- The Problem
- Context-aware Positioning Model
- Next Steps

Daniel Moreno, SADUE'13   2

What is Positioning?

- Basically, positioning addresses the problem of knowing the position of an asset in a physical environment.

- Positioning Strategies:
  - Triangulation
  - Proximity
  - Fingerprinting
  - Scene Analysis

Daniel Moreno, SADUE'13   3

Positioning Strategies

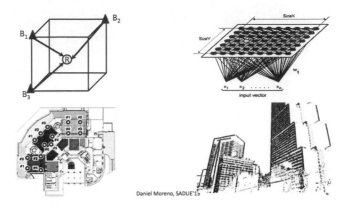

Daniel Moreno, SADUE'13

Positioning Scenarios

Daniel Moreno, SADUE'13   5

Scenario's Context Variability

- Users are frequently on the move while performing their activities, so their context is continuously changing.

- Mobile Ad-hoc networks (MANETs) allow mobile devices to communicate and share information.

- Ubiquitous positioning applications should be able to detect context changes and self-adapt their behavior accordingly.

Daniel Moreno, SADUE'13   6

Ubiquitous Positioning

- The goal is to allow users to determine their current location anywhere, whenever they require it.

- Depending on the positioning strategy being used and the accuracy requirement, this could be quite costly in terms of
  - Network traffic
  - Energy

Ubiquitous Positioning Issues

- **Mobility**: Users move through indoor and outdoor scenarios indistinctively while pursuing their interests.

- **Energy**: A valuable asset that is not always readily available for mobile users for extended periods of time.

- **Available Instrumentation**: Not all environments allow the use of the same techniques.

- **Participants' Capabilities**: The ambient-sensing and positioning capabilities of the devices are varied.

The Problem

- How to enable all participants in a given environment, including those with no positioning capabilities of their own, to *know their position*?

- How to allow the participants a *transparent swap* between positioning systems, in any scenario?

- How to achieve the former while *minimizing the energy consumption* of the participants?

Our Proposal

- We aim to define a **context-aware indoor-outdoor positioning model** that allows devices to determine their position within seven meters in any scenario, involving low energy consumption.

- The model will also provide a smooth transition between available positioning services on the go, independent of the current scenario.

Layer-based Context-aware Positioning Model

1.3. Context-aware Positioning Method
1.2. Context Information Management
1.1. Ambient Sensing

Layer-based Context-aware Positioning Model

- The *ambient sensing* layer determines which context variables to sense and how to do it.

- The *context information management* layer stores and manages the context information related to the user's current environment, the positioning strategies that can be used on it, and the peer collaboration algorithms.

- The *context-aware positioning method* layer uses the context information to determine which positioning strategy to use in each case.

Our work so far

- The first stage of this proposal is related to the *Ambient Sensing* layer of the Positioning Model.

- Up to now, we have:
  - selected sets of context variables that will be used to characterize the environment and the devices.
  - designed a simulation scenario that mimics real world indoor and outdoor scenarios to perform the required tests.

Contextual Characterization

- Scenario
  - *Access Points* (amount, strength)
  - *Positioning Strategies* (availability, confidence)
  - *Peers* (amount, capabilities)
  - *Obstacles*

- Devices
  - *Network Communication* (protocols, data transmission)
  - *Positioning Capabilities* (Sensors, positioning strategies)
  - *Energy*
  - *Position*

Characterization of the Scenario

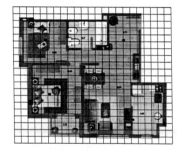 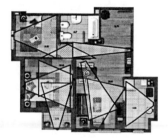

Characterization of Devices

- **High Priority**: knows its position with high certainty, has high energy levels, or has increased sensing or communication capabilities.

- **Medium Priority**: has average values for the context variables.

- **Low Priority**: doesn't know its position, has low energy levels, cannot sense the environment, or has reduced communication capabilities.

Daniel Moreno, SADUE'13   16

But... what does this mean?

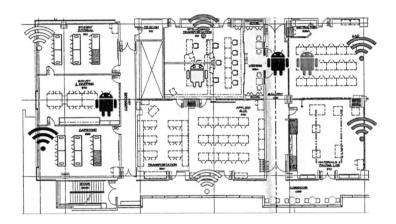

Choosing the best strategy

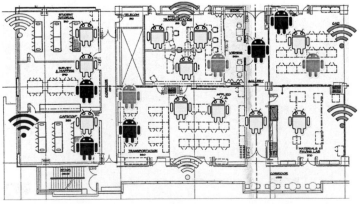

Transparent Strategy Swap

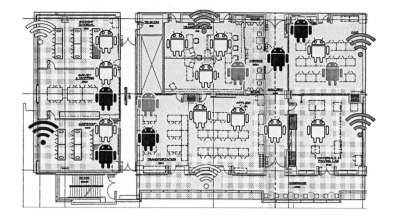

Simulation Scenario

- We have used the Network Simulator (NS2, a discrete event simulator targeted at networking research) to emulate the interaction of network accesses and mobile devices in a controlled environment.

- The NS2 provides substantial support for simulation of TCP, routing, and multicast protocols over wired and wireless networks, and allows modding via users' scripts to add new functionalities.

Real World Scenario

- Currently we are in the process of measuring signals in the third floor of the DCC building, to use as a ground truth that would allow us to fine tune the simulation's parameters.

So... now what?

- Define a strategy for context information management, to allow the model to determine the available positioning strategy with better results and lower energy consumption.

- Formalize the former strategy into the context-aware positioning model.

- Test it!

Thank you for your attention!

- Any question or suggestion is welcome.

Mobile and Ubiquitous Computing: A Brief Summary of Current Projects

Sergio F. Ochoa

Department of Computer Science, Universidad de Chile
Av. Blanco Encalada 2120, 3rd Floor, Santiago, Chile.
sochoa@dcc.uchile.cl

Abstract. In recent years, the massive adoption of mobile computing devices has presented many opportunities for mobile and ubiquitous computing. This talk presents a brief summary of some current research projects being conducted by members of the Computer Science Department at the University of Chile. These projects address problems that range from the social isolation affecting older adults to urban emergency response. Here, we describe these projects and the results obtained to date.

Keywords: Mobile computing, ubiquitous computing, system design, application scenario

1 Introduction

Today most people (from children to elders) count on a mobile computing device with communication capabilities (e.g., cellular phones, iPads and netbook/notebook/ tablet PCs). Typically, these devices support our personal and/or working activities, such as coordinating a meeting (through voice/text message exchange), sharing files (through data message exchange), or just working while we are on the move. In other words, we use mobile computing devices as portable versions of traditional desktop computers and telephones. However, mobile devices have the potential to go a step further in facilitating our day-to-day activities at home, in the workplace, and on the go.

Examples of services that can be provided by these devices, particularly cellular phones, are the following: (1) locating persons in a physical environment while they are on the move (e.g., a nurse looking for a physician in a hospital or a mother looking for her children in a crowded place), (2) knowing the current availability of a person before trying to conduct a face-to-face interaction with him/her (e.g., a medical intern waiting for the opinion of a specialist), and (3) exchanging or synchronizing information when two mobile users meet on the street (e.g., a salesman delivering a file containing a product list to a customer). We envision that these types of services can positively impact the activities of mobile users (including children, elders, and most mobile workers). However, how to maximize this potential is not clear.

Given our poor understanding of the relationship between mobile computing solutions, nomadic workers' productivity, and technology adoption (including acceptance), more research is needed in this area, If we understand how to manage the relationship among these variables, we will be able to consistently diagnose the impact of these solutions on any work scenario, including healthcare, security, productivity, business, education, emergency response processes, and social work.

In trying to address these challenges, we are conducting several research activities in various application scenarios. The next section presents a summary of most of these projects and the results we have obtained so far.

2 Summary of the Current Projects

Five research projects are briefly described in this section in order to present our research interests and to try to find collaborators to advance the state of the art in these areas. Although many people are doing research in mobile and ubiquitous computing, a greater effort is required if we are to address the long list of questions that are still unanswered. These are the research projects that we are currently conducting in the Computer Science Department of the University of Chile:

2.1 Social Inclusion of Older Adults in the Digital Media Age

In the early 1990s, social interactions were supported mainly by telephone and face-to-face communication. However, the rise of the Internet and ubiquitous computing has diversified the interaction mechanisms people use to socialize. Typically, young people tend to prefer social networking services, adults prefer e-mail or telephone, and elders prefer face-to-face communication.

Usually, there are also differences in the time periods in which people need to or can socialize with others. Although this interaction asymmetry is present in almost all scenarios where the participants belong to different generations, it is particularly relevant in familial communities since they are dependent on social interaction. In these communities, the most vulnerable members are the elders; the interaction asymmetry coupled with elders' reluctance to use digital media may cause social isolation and thus negatively affect their physical and mental health. To help overcome this problem, our research seeks to design computer-based mechanisms to reduce the asymmetry. Our work will focus on elders and reducing the asymmetry between them and the rest of their family. The interim results of this project are available in [10, 11].

2.2 Supporting Casual Encounters Among Acquaintances

Mobile computing provides ubiquitous access to social networking services, allowing computer-mediated interaction among their members. However, people still prefer face-to-face social interaction. In this project, we have developed a new and complementary interaction paradigm promoting face-to-face encounters among community members based on their physical proximity and using mobile devices.

This hybrid (i.e., physical and digital) interaction paradigm was implemented in a ubiquitous application called Lukap [14]. Although other applications have been proposed to support or promote face-to-face interaction among community members, none of them are able to do so ubiquitously. Lukap not only promotes physical interaction, but does so without requiring access to infrastructure-based communication networks or SNS. It is expected that an application like Lukap will help increase the number of face-to-face interactions, thus maintaining long-term relationships [3], developing trust among members [15], and improving people's mental health [4].

The Lukap evaluation results indicate that the user interface does not properly fit the mental model of end users; therefore, it requires improvement. Nevertheless, the results indicate that the application is perceived as useful to support face-to-face encounters.

The performance evaluation results indicate that the application is able to detect users quickly when they are up to two hops away and in an acceptable time when there are up to three hops away. Thus, the application provides an appropriate coverage area to support these encounters—up to 60 meters in built-up areas and up to 300 meters in open areas.

The communication throughput of the application is good enough to allow developers to implement several interaction mechanisms between the users. The results obtained in this project are available in [14].

2.3 Enhancing Personal Security

Violence and crime in large urban areas are an ongoing problem worldwide. The current mechanisms to provide personal security are not particularly focused on helping potential victims easily determine their personal risk in real time, thus diminishing their ability to take appropriate and timely preventive action. To help address that problem, we have designed and implemented a participatory sensing system that complements the solutions already used by government organizations. The system is based on a human-centric wireless sensor network. It uses crowdsourcing, human-based sensors, and regular sensors to collect information from the field as well as various awareness mechanisms to inform users of their current personal security risks. The information provided by the system can also be used to build a spatiotemporal view of crime (e.g., by incident type) that allows security organizations to understand its evolution and to improve crime fighting and crime prevention.

The usability of the system was evaluated using two different techniques. The results allowed us to identify the need to adjust some components of the user interface, even though they were minor issues. System performance and the pertinence of the warnings given by the application have not been formally evaluated at this stage. However, they were indirectly assessed through the activity test performed by the evaluators. Our preliminary findings indicate that these aspects of the solution lie at least among the expected values for such systems. These results are reported in [2].

2.4 Sharing Displays to Support Informal Meetings

Shared displays have shown to be useful in supporting informal meetings in various scenarios, such as at home, in hospitals or in business settings. Every day it becomes increasingly important to smoothly integrate the mobile devices used by meeting participants and the large displays available in the physical environment. This integration could allow participants to share and analyze the supporting information in a faster or more effective way.

In this project we developed a framework called Clairvoyance, which provides a smooth integration between shared displays (particularly large-screen TVs and computer screens) and mobile devices (particularly smartphones and laptops). The main goal of this framework is to help people share visual resources during informal meetings or social encounters without having to connect devices physically (e.g., with cables) or perform device configuration processes. The solution uses a wireless link between a shared display and the mobile device that deploys the visual information; moreover, the integration is transparent for meeting participants. No infrastructure-based communication networks are required in the environment where this solution is used since Clairvoyance automatically creates and manages the communication links required to perform the operations.

This framework provides an API with several user services that can be utilized by software developers to create solutions that support informal meetings in particular scenarios. These services were used by two software engineers to develop a ubiquitous application supporting social encounters between friends or relatives. Although this evaluation is not sufficient to draw final conclusions, preliminary results indicate that Clairvoyance services are reusable as well as helpful and easy to use for developers of such solutions.

Clairvoyance's performance was evaluated in certain settings as a means of assessing how reliable and stable its services are. The results allowed us to identify some improvement areas; however, the service's performance and reliability are currently good enough to support informal meetings.

Finally, the application was evaluated by end users in two instances. The first involved a list of activities for users to perform individually using the system. The results were encouraging, with all participants being able to complete the activities. Young people in particular were highly enthusiastic about using the application, and this group of users performed best.

The second evaluation involved two groups of people performing a real informal meeting—a social encounter to share travel pictures. The participants utilized most of the Clairvoyance services and also decided when to use them. The results showed that users were more enthusiastic about the system than in the previous evaluation instance. Since the Clairvoyance user interface is simple, an ample range of people were able to use it successfully. The current results of this project were reported in [1].

2.5 Supporting Responses to Urban Emergencies

Information communication support is a serious limitation for firefighters when they deal with urban emergency situations. The insufficient number of radio channels available and the inability to access digital information force firefighters to improvise during response processes; for example, they must make decisions based solely on their experience but with only poor supporting information or none at all. These improvised actions affect the time required to take control of a crisis situation as well as its evolution.

In this project we have developed several research studies and also software platforms and applications to support firefighters' activities during the response process. The most import application we developed for this work scenario was MobileMap [7], which is the result of the research and development work conducted by the authors, supported by a Chilean fire company, in the course of the last three years. MobileMap is a low-cost mobile collaborative application that can be used in emergency situations to overcome most of the firefighters' communication problems. It allows ad hoc communication, decision support, and collaboration among firefighters in the field using mobile devices. This solution complements radio communication systems. Since the interactions supported by MobileMap are recorded, it is possible to analyze this information after the crisis and use this analysis to prepare for future emergencies. The tool was evaluated in simulated and real scenarios, and the results are highly encouraging. The results of the various studies were reported in [5, 6, 7, 8, 9, 12, 13].

Acknowledgements

These projects are partially funded by the Fondecyt Project (Chile), grants 1120207; the LACCIR project, grant R1210LAC002; and the European Commission, FP7-PEOPLE-2012-IRSES, grant 316337.

References

1. Berkhoff, C., Ochoa, S.F., Pino, J.A., Favela, J., Oliveira, J., and Guerrero, L.A.: Clairvoyance: A Framework to Integrate Shared Displays and Mobile Computing Devices. Future Generation Computer Systems. In Press, to appear in 2014
2. Carreño, P., Gutierrez, F., Ochoa, S.F., and Fortino, G.: Using Human-centric Wireless Sensor Networks to Support Personal Security. Proceedings of the 6th International Conference on Internet and Distributed Computing Systems (IDCS 2013), LNCS 8223, pp. 51–64. Hangzhou, Zhejiang, China. Oct. 28th-30th, 2013
3. D'Aprix, R.: The Face-to-Face Communication Toolkit: Creating an Engaged Workforce. IABC Press, San Francisco (2009)
4. Goffman, E.: The Presentation of Self in Everyday Life. Anchor Books, New York (1959)
5. Ibarra, M., Monares, A., Ochoa, S.F., and Pino, J.A.: Reducing Radio Traffic in Urban Emergencies with a Mobile Collaborative Application. Proceedings of the 2012 16th IEEE International Conference on Computer Supported Cooperative Work in Design (CSCWD2012), Wuhan, China. May 23–25, 2012
6. Ibarra, M.J., Monares, A., Ochoa, S.F., and Pino, J.A.: A Strategy for Selecting Points of Interest on Mobile Devices for Emergency Situations. CLEI Electronic Journal 17(3), paper no. 05, December 2013
7. Monares, A. Ochoa, S.F., Pino, J.A., Herskovic, V., Rodriguez-Covili, J., and Neyem, A.: Mobile Computing in Urban Emergency Situations: Improving the Support to Firefighters in the Field. Expert Systems with Applications 38(2), 1255–1267 (2011)

8. Monares, A., Ochoa, S.F., Pino, J.A., and Herskovic, V.: Improving the Initial Response Process in Urban Emergencies. Proceedings of the 2012 16th IEEE International Conference on Computer Supported Cooperative Work in Design (CSCWD2012), Wuhan, China. May 23 –25, 2012

9. Monares, A., Ochoa, S.F., Pino, J.A., Ruiz-Lopez, T., and Noguera, M.: Using Unconventional Awareness Mechanisms to Support Mobile Work. Proceedings of ChileCHI'13, ACM Press. Temuco, Chile. November 11–15, 2013

10. Muñoz, D., Cornejo, R., Ochoa, S.F., Favela, J., Gutierrez, F., and Tentori, M.: Aligning Intergenerational Communication Patterns and Rhythms in the Age of Social Media. Proc. of the 1st Chilean Conference on Human-Computer Interaction (ChileCHI'13), ACM Press. Temuco, Chile (2013)

11. Muñoz, D., Gutierrez, F., Ochoa, S.F., and Baloian, N.: Enhancing Social Interaction between Older Adults and Their Families. Proc. of the 5th International Work-Conference on Ambient Assisted Living (IWAAL'13). Guanacaste, Costa Rica (2013)

12. Ochoa, S.F., Santos, R.: Human-centric Wireless Sensor Networks to Improve Information Availability During Urban Search and Rescue Activities. Information Fusion. DOI: http://dx.doi.org/10.1016/j.inffus.2013.05.009, In press, to appear in 2014

13. Suarez, D., Monares, A., Ochoa, S.F., Pino, J.A., and Ibarra, M.: Improving the Support to Decision Making in Medium-sized Urban Emergencies. Proc. of the 17th IEEE International Conference on Computer-Supported Cooperative Work in Design (CSCWD'13), pp. 251–256. Whistler, B.C., Canada, June 27–29, 2013

14. Vergara, C., Ochoa, S.F., Gutierrez, F., and Rodriguez-Covili, J.F.: Extending Social Networking Services toward a Physical Interaction Scenario. Proceedings of the 6th International Conference on Ubiquitous Computing and Ambient Intelligence (UCAmI 2012), LNCS 7656, pp. 208–215. Vitoria-Gasteiz, Spain, Dec. 3–5, 2012

15. Westerlund, M., Rajala, R., Nykänen, K., and Järvensivu, T.: Trust and Commitment in Social Networking: Lessons Learned from Two Empirical Studies. Proceedings of the 25th IMP Conference. Marseille, France, 2009

Mobile and Ubiquitous Computing: A Brief Summary of the Current Projects

Sergio F. Ochoa
Computer Science Department,
University of Chile
sochoa@dcc.uchile.cl

August 2013

Outline

- **Social Isolation**

- **Casual Encounters**

- **Personal Security**

- **Shared Displays**

- **Emergency Responses**

- **Some Conclusions**

2

Social Isolation

Social Connector – An Exploratory Case Study

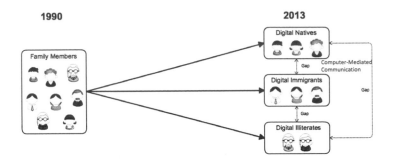

1990   2013

Social Isolation – A First RQ

- How to integrate elders to the CMC age?

- ... most of them use telephone.

- An exploratory prototype: the Social Connector

Social Connector

Social Connector

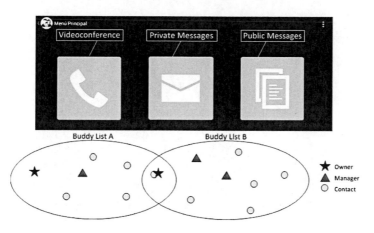

Social Connector – Basic Architecture

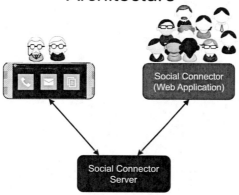

Social Connector

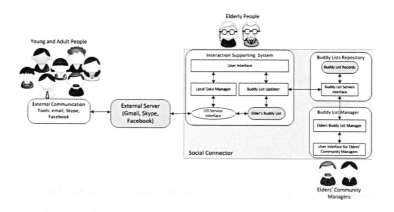

Social Connector

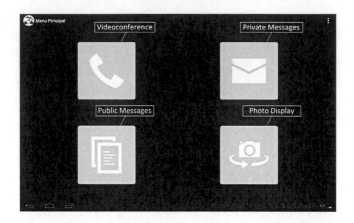

Social Connector

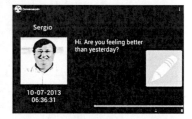

Social Connector – Detecting Emotions

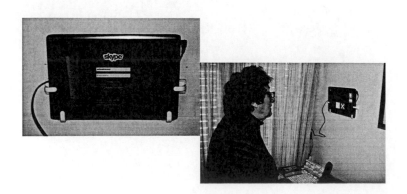

Casual Encounters

Main Goal: Increase the opportunities to perform face-to-face social interactions.

Casual Encounters

14

Casual Encounters

Lukap!: Importing Contacts

Lukap!: Casual Encounters

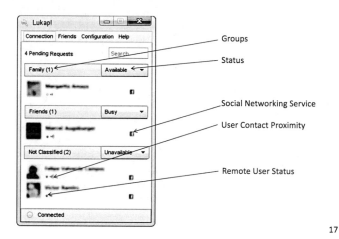

Lukap!: Positioning

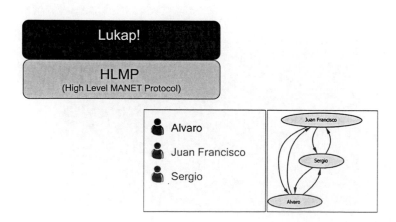

Preliminary Results: Usability Evaluation

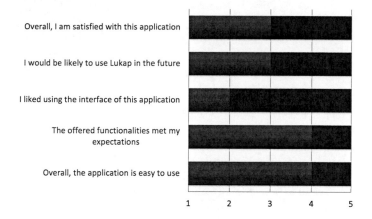

Preliminary Results:
Performance Evaluation

	1-hop	2-hops	3-hops	4-hops
Maximum delay for user detection	6 sec.	8 sec.	17 sec.	92 sec.
Percentage of detection fails	0%	0%	20%	60%
Communication throughput	127 Kb	87 Kb	42 Kb	14 Kb

Enhancing the Personal Security of Citizens

Goal: Make people aware of their personal security level while they move around urban areas. Thus, we intend to reduce their vulnerability to be victims of delinquency.

Enhancing the Personal Security of Citizens

- How can we **prevent crime**?

    - Using surveillance cameras.
    - Increasing the presence of security agents in the field.

    These solutions do not have **good scalability**, because it is not feasible to flood a city with surveillance cameras or police personnel that can be active at all times protecting civilians.

    22

Motivation

The current mechanisms to provide personal security **are not particularly focused on helping potential victims easily determine their inherent risk to crimes in real-time...**

.... therefore their capability to take appropriate and on-time preventive actions is diminished

23

Motivation

- How can we prevent crime?

    Involve citizens to a greater extent: increase the coverage area and the monitoring capability of security organizations.

24

Participatory Sensing

"Task deployed mobile devices to form interactive, participatory sensor networks that enable public and professional users to gather, analyze and share local knowledge" [Burke et al., 2006]

25

Participatory Sensing

- Sensors in mobile devices (smartphones)
  - Motion sensor / Accelerometer
  - Gyroscope
  - Ambient light sensor

- These sensors have made participatory sensing **viable in the large-scale.**

26

Human-centric Wireless Sensor Networks

- Layered architecture to support participatory sensing [Estrin, 2010]

- **Mobile units**: intermediary between servers and sensors, which can eventually support asynchronous communication [Duarte et al., 2013]

- **Witness units**: information repository for users located in a particular area [Ochoa & Santos, 2014]

27

Implemented System

Implemented System

Information form	Map display	Risk display
the Human-based Sensor indicates what event they saw or suffered, when it happened, and how many times they have seen similar situations in that place	shows the user current location and the records of incidents within 200 meters	information displayed to the user when a risk overcome a certain threshold

Usability Evaluation

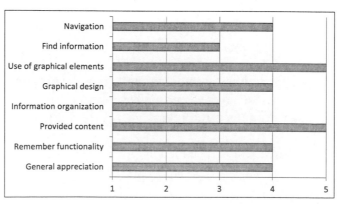

Usability Evaluation

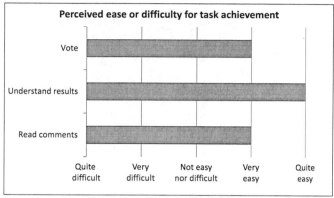

Perceived ease or difficulty for task achievement

	Quite difficult	Very difficult	Not easy nor difficult	Very easy	Quite easy

Vote

Understand results

Read comments

31

Shared Displays

Sharing Small Displays

-125-

Clairvoyance: For Smooth Integration of Large-screen TVs and Mobile Devices

Clairvoyance: Architecture of the Physical Environment

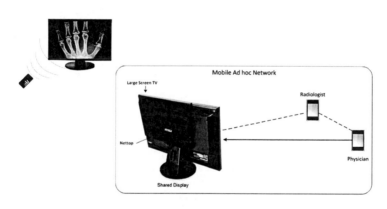

HLMP–based Solutions

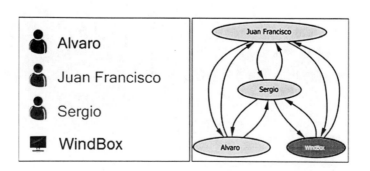

Clairvoyance: User Interface

Evaluation Results: Usability, Usefulness & Performance

Evaluation Item	Smartphone		Laptop		Signif.
	Avg.	Std. Dev.	Avg.	Std. Dev.	p
How suitable was the response time shown by the application	3.9	0.69	4.6	0.55	0.08
How understandable were the user interfaces of the system	4.3	0.76	4.4	0.55	0.44
How useful were the system services to perform the required actions	4.6	0.53	3.8	0.45	0.63
How reliable were the services provided by the system	4.7	0.49	4.6	0.55	0.61

Evaluation Results: Usability, Usefulness & Performance

Users Age	Laptop and Smartphone		CI95%	
	# of Participants	Avg. Time	Lower Limit	Upper Limit
G1: 10-15 years old	3	7.3 min.	5.97 min.	9.23 min.
G2: 18-25 years old	4	8.4 min.	7.45 min.	8.9 min.
G3: 42-45 years old	3	17.2 min.	8.44 min.	23.3 min.
G4: 56-60 years old	3	16.1 min.	11.62 min.	28.05 min.

Urban Emergency Support

Context

Medium-Sized Emergencies: Response processes taking between *six to ten hours* or involving *six to twelve fire trucks*.

| Landsides | Fires in Factories | Multiple-vehicle Collisions |

Emergency Response Process

1) Emergency

2) Notification

3) Verification

4) Resources Assignment

5) Definition of an Incident Comander

6) Decision Making (Response Actions)

7) Monitoring and Evaluation

8) Closure

Problem to Address

The information exchange saturates the communication channel

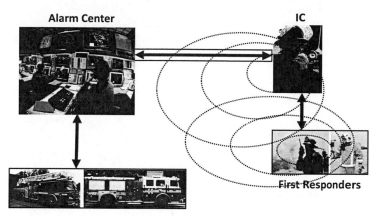

Problem to Address

- Lack of available radio channels

- Communication interference

- Lack of support for sharing digital information

Lack of Information to Make Decisions

Improvisation

A Decentralized Decision Support System

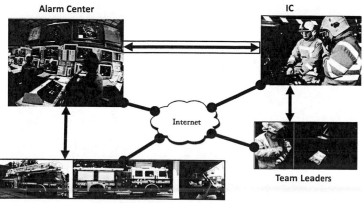

Conception and Plan

- Three Focus Groups and 34 medium-sized urban emergencies were analyzed.

Msg. Code	Meaning	# of Emergencies	# of Msg	% of Emergencies
0-5	Emergency location	21	32	62%
0-5	Location of fire trucks	32	149	94%
—	Which trucks were assigned to the emergency?	11	25	32%
6-8	Fire trucks available	9	9	26%
6-5	Location of nearby hydrants	22	53	65%
7-0	Command post is established	22	29	65%
—	What truck is missing in there?	4	13	12%
7-1	Indicate emergency information	22	26	65%
7-2	Indicate fire trucks information	6	17	18%
—	Time of ambulance	3	4	9%
0-5	Pool (open water)	3	3	9%

System Implementation

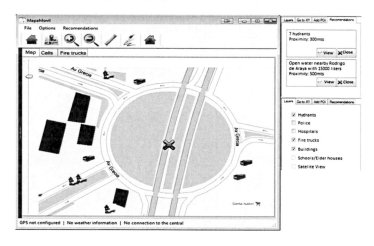

Some Conclusions…

- It is a **Quite New Area** that Requires Exploration and Learning.

- This is just the **Starting Point**.

- There are **Social, Psychological** and **Organizational Issues** that should be considered.

- Work on **Systems' Usability** is mandatory.

- The **Work Context** for these systems is highly relevant, but it is not easy to address.

48

Cultural Heritage in Metropolitan Areas Using a Virtual Museum Framework

Daniel Biella

Center for Information and Media Services (CIM),
University of Duisburg-Essen,
Forsthausweg 2, 47048 Duisburg, Germany
daniel.biella@uni-due.de

Abstract. This talk highlights the role of smart museums and their objects in the Internet of Things and gives an overview of the ViMEDEAS virtual museum framework. Finally, two best practices from the cultural heritage domain are presented, proving the usability of this software and visualization framework for use cases in the metropolitan areas of Santiago de Chile (Chile) and the Rhine-Ruhr region (Germany).

Keywords: virtual museums, information visualization, smart museums

1 Smart Museums and the Internet of Things

The principle of the Internet of Things (IoT) is essential to many smart applications. As soon as an object ("thing") can communicate information about itself, it has the potential to become a smart object and, therefore, part of the IoT. What if this principle is applied to domains other than sensors and actors? What if the idea of the IoT is applied to abstract domains or concepts?

Consider the concept "library." One of the basic objects contained in a library is books. Thus, defining books as "things," unique identifiers, such as ISBN or DOI, can reference them, and standards like DublinCore can describe their content and context; this is true for both virtual and real books. Due to the existence of these unique identification codes and established metadata standards, books can be easily identified as parts of an IoT despite their lack of sensors.

Now consider the concept "museum." A museum may contain many different basic objects, such as paintings, sculptures, installations, or even virtual-only art. The high degree of diversity among "art objects" is one of the reasons why there is no commonly used unique identification code scheme as there is for books (i.e., ISBN). And unlike most books, many art objects can have numerous tempo-spatial states. Modern light installations change their shape interactively and "by design" (e.g., Strømmer installation, Norway); Joseph Beuys's famous *Fat Corner* would easily melt away if certain environmental conditions applied; art works can be modified by renovation or preservation actions; they can be the result of inspiration by another art work or artist; and they can be modified by (mostly undesired) exterior factors, such as fire, water, or other damage. In summary, the current metadata schemes for art objects have limited description capabilities for the above-mentioned types of art and for hybrid—that is, both virtual and real—art objects.

2 The ViMEDEAS Framework

The Virtual Museum Exhibition Designer Using Enhanced ARCO Standard (ViMEDEAS) was developed with three main goals in mind: (1) to define a workflow-based digitization pipeline, (2) to develop a metadata standard to meet the above-mentioned shortcomings, and (3) to create a rendering engine (i.e., a parameterizable X3D code generator). Talks and discussion with curators showed that a software must feature a high degree of intuitive usability.

ViMEDEAS is a software portfolio for the creation and publication of X3D Web museums supported by the development of a metadata standard with a focus on 3D; it is based on the ARCO standard and other existing metadata standards. The workflow includes four major steps: (1) digitization/acquisition, (2) room design/object allocation, (3) museum design, and (4) visualization.

In step 1 objects are either digitized using geometric modeling (or existing models) or 3D scanning, including 2D or 3D textures. After that, each object is finalized with a ViMCOX-based metadata description file. This step results in an X3D file(s), a ViMCOX file, and (optionally) texture files. By design, ViMEDEAS is not a geometric modeling tool. Users can use any modeler supporting X3D code export (e.g., Blender, X3D-Edit).

In step 2 a 3D room can be designed with a 2D modeling tool, a room designer. (Using 2D.decreases the complexity of the GUI) Optionally, an existing room layout can be imported. Next, one or more objects (generated in step 1) are allocated to a specific room. As a result, the ViMCOX file is enhanced by n room node elements. The corresponding object files from step 1 are taken over.

In step 3, existing rooms can be imported into the museum editor. Here, selected rooms (from step 2) can be logically aligned to a virtual museum space by placing thresholds in an 8-neighborhood manner. Basically, these thresholds are bidirectional URL anchors in both adjoined rooms. As a result, the selected room (and object) elements of the ViMCOX file of step 2 are taken over, with added museum data elements based on the ViMCOX standard.

In step 4, the Replicave2 framework is used to render X3D code from a generated ViMCOX-compatible XML file (e.g., mymuseum.xml) using all other assets and information described or generated in the previous steps.

3 Case Studies in Metropolitan Areas

The technology described and presented here has been successfully used in case studies in metropolitan regions. In 2010 a room in the Muséo de Arte Contemporáneo (MAC) in Santiago de Chile (Chile) was digitized as a windowless indoor exhibition room. In 2013 the virtual Fleischhacker museum was completed, showing a mix of real and reconstructed art, various object types, and different object environments (indoor and outdoor). The museum also includes a guided tour and is being prepared for a hands-on on-site interactive terminal installation at a heritage site.

4 Outlook

Recent activities include the porting of the room designer to the Android platform. Up to now, a total of 19 theses have been written on aspects of ViMEDEAS. Future research will focus on, among other things, the following:

- Questions of 3D data acquisition (use of consumer-class products, crowd-based approach)
- Extension of the metadata standard ViMCOX
- User-friendly software ("3D-to-go")
- Reusability of content (repository, DRM, information retrieval)
- Support for mobile devices (location services, visualization, data acquisition, path tracking, guided tour, etc.)
- Replicave (increase of customizability)

Open questions include the following:

- Integration of recommender systems and approaches
- Collaborative filtering
- Open data collections
- Cooperation with museums:
  - Guided tours (or tour guides) with indoor navigation
  - Reconstruction and modeling of exhibition rooms
  - Evaluation (semi-automatically generated vs. reconstructed rooms)
  - Add-on material, supplements

Cultural heritage in metropolitan areas using a virtual museum framework

Keywords: virtual museums, information visualization, smart museums

Dr Daniel Biella, SADUE13 Workshop, Santiago de Chile

Zentrum für Informations- und Mediendienste

TOC

Part 1: Smart museums and the Internet of things

„Ideas and information are important, but things matter much more. Yet today's information technology is so dependent on data originated by people that our computers know more about ideas than things. If we had computers that knew everything there was to know about things – using data they gathered without any help from us – we would be able to track and count everything, and greatly reduce waste, loss and cost.“

– Kevin Ashton, 2009

„Library"
contains

referenced by
ISBN, DOI
described by e.g.
DublinCore

„Library"
contains

referenced by
ISBN, DOI
described by e.g.
DublinCore

„Museum"
contains

referenced by
„some id"
described by e.g.
ARCO, Spectrum,...

And, what if...

„Museum"
contains

Shortcomings in existing Metadata-Standards

- **Limited support for hybrid description of both virtual and real art objects**
- **Limited description capabilities for *stateful* art objects**
  - User interaction and supported methods „by design" (Strømmer)
  - Environment-related states (Fatty corner)
  - Maintenance-related states (preservation)
  - Extensions ("forked" art)
  - Other states (unintentional, e.g. fire, damage)

Tasks at hand

- **Develop and implement a metadata standard for virtual museums and cultural objects (vimcox.xsd)**
- **Develop and implement a visualization framework (Replicave)**
- **Develop a digitization pipeline (workflow)**
- **Develop and implement additional tools and bundle (ViMEDEAS)**

Part 2: The Vimedeas framework and its concepts

- **The Vimedeas framework and its concepts**
  - The digitization pipeline
  - The Vimcox Metadata standard
  - The rendering engine Replicave

Interactive and ubiquitous presentation of cultural heritage & art objects via the web, for:

- Education
- Marketing (appetizer)
- Planning and documentation of art exhibitions
- Facilitate cooperations
- Evaluation

Challenges/requirements:

- Digitization of 3D content
- Intuitive software
- Metadata…

- **Software portfolio for creation and publication of X3D web museums**
- **Development of a metadata standard with focus on 3D, based on ARCO and others (Vimcox 1.2)**
- **Work flow:**

| Digitisation/ Acquisition | → | Room design/ object allocation | → | Museum design | → | Visualisation |

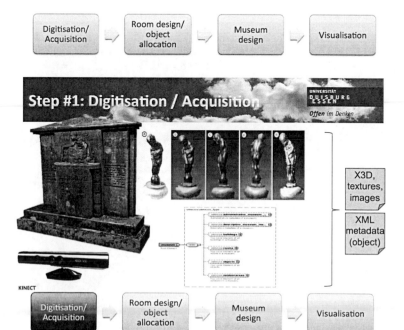

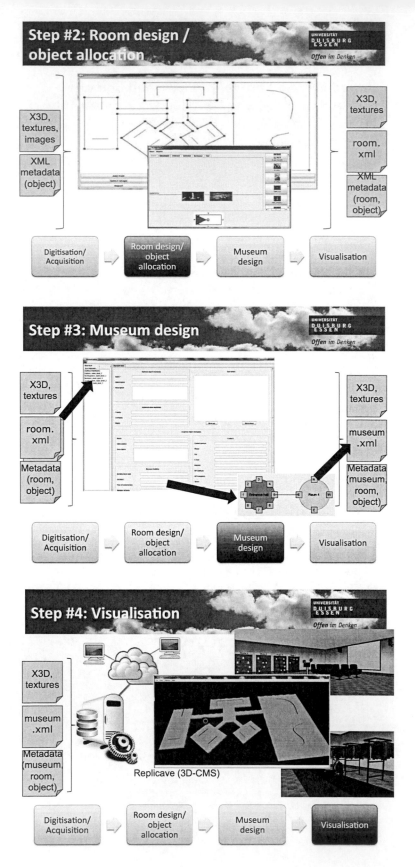

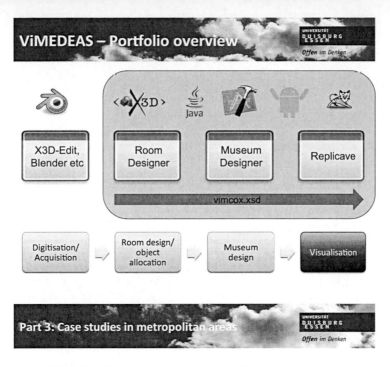

Part 3: Case studies in metropolitan areas

- ## Muséo de arte contemporáneo
    - Real museum, real objects
    - Objects located in Santiago de Chile, Chile
    - 3D reproduction of real museum
- ## Virtual Fleischhacker Museum
    - Virtual museum, real and virtual-only objects
    - Objects are or were located in the Rhine-Ruhr area, Germany (Düsseldorf, Duisburg, Krefeld)
    - Feasibility of outdoor scenarios, virtual exhibition

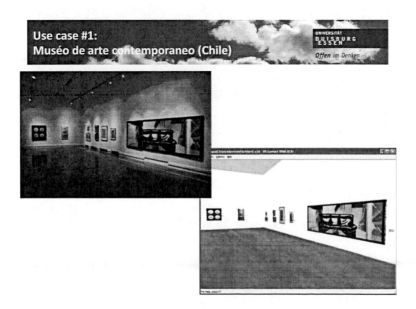

Use case #1:
Muséo de arte contemporaneo (Chile)

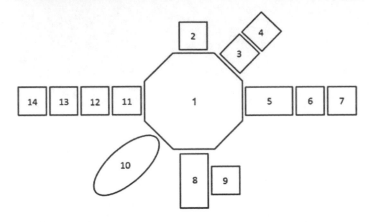

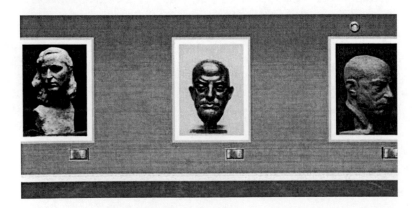

Use case #2: The virtual Fleischhacker museum (Rhine-Ruhr area)

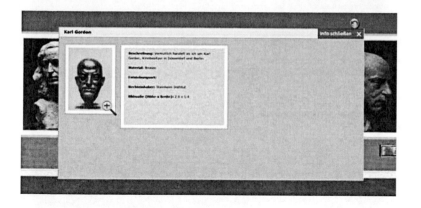

Use case #2: The virtual Fleischhacker museum (Rhine-Ruhr area)

Use case #2: The virtual Fleischhacker museum (Rhine-Ruhr area)

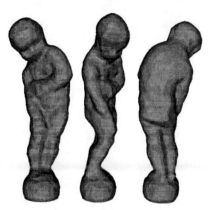

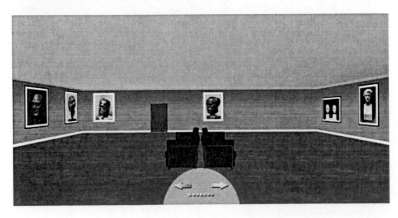

- Recent activities
- Open questions
- Discussion

- **Virtual 3D museum w/ objects by German sculptor L. Fleischhacker (outdoor scenario, sculptures), Terminal installation planned**
- **Mobile room designer app (01/13)**
- **MS Kinect in 3D data acquisition (01/13)**
- **#theses (total): 19**

Open questions

- 3D data acquisition (usage of consumer class products, crowd based approach)
- Extension of metadata standard Vimcox
- User-friendly software ("3D-to-go")
- Reusability of content (repository, DRM, information retrieval)
- Support for mobile devices (location services, visualisation, data acquisition, path tracking, guided tour,...)
- Replicave (increase customizability)

Open questions

- **Recommender systems**
- **Collaborative Filtering**
- **Open Data Collections**
- **Cooperations with museums:**
  - Guided tours (or tour guides) with indoor navigation
  - Reconstruction and modelling of exhibition rooms
  - Evaluation (semi-automatically generated vs. reconstructed rooms)
  - Add-on material, supplements

Thanks for your attention

Acknowledgements

Many thanks to our project partners from the Salomon Ludwig Steinheim-Institut and our students; Henrik Detjen, Marco Janc, Simon Leßmann, Dominic Ripkens, Sabine Steffen, Markus Stolzenburg, Lukas Stukenbrock and Serdar Yaslar for their valuable summaries; careful implementation of the software; provision of 3D models, textures and screenshots; and building The Virtual Leopold Fleischhacker Museum.

And, of course,...http://www.vimeadeas.com/

Virtual Museums:
From Content Creation to Presentation

Daniel Sacher

Department of Computer Science and Applied Cognitive Science (INKO),
University of Duisburg-Essen, Germany
daniel.sacher@uni-due.de

Keywords: ViMEDEAS, ViMCOX, Replicave, Metadata, Virtual Museum, 3D Framework, X3D, X3Dom

1 The Curator Software Suite ViMEDEAS

In this paper, we describe the modeling and 3D visualization capabilities of the curator software suite Virtual Museum Exhibition Designer Using an Enhanced ARCO Standard (ViMEDEAS) for presenting digitized heritage sites or virtual museums with access to outdoor areas ([1], [2], [3], [4]). As visualization platforms—for local or for online presentation—we utilize the ISO standard X3D as a format as well as HTML5, WebGL, and X3Dom [3]. The metadata format used to model the exhibition areas, virtual landscapes, and heritage sites is the Virtual Museum and Cultural Object Exchange Format (ViMCOX) [5], which is included in ViMEDEAS. ViMCOX was developed to support the hierarchical description of virtual museums and provides stylistic devices for sophisticated and vivid exhibition design, which cannot be achieved using classic museum standards. ViMCOX supports interactive exhibition content, assets, out-door areas, and spatial exhibition design, including illumination concepts as well as free and guided virtual museum tours [4].

The metadata format ViMCOX is based on international metadata standards and uses LIDO (Lightweight Information Describing Objects) version 1.0 as an interchange and harvesting format for cultural objects. The key idea is to have a common modeling language specification that is capable of structuring and presenting virtual 3D museums and that outlives rapidly changing technological trends. Thus, content creators and developers choose freely among authoring tools, use different operating systems, and apply a variety of graphic libraries to target even mobile platforms. ViMCOX facilitates the abstract and declarative description of content as well as dynamic metadata-based generation of exhibitions, interiors, and room layouts with the advantage of detached processes and tailored application-specific metadata.

2 Architectural Design

The architectural design of exhibition areas can be defined by specifying the dimensions of a room as a bounding box, by specifying a 2D floor plan to define custom room shapes with parameters for geometric windows or doors, or by re-using 3D environmental models as exhibition space or out-door areas. In addition, content creators can vary the lighting of exhibition areas. ViMCOX distinguishes between two light source terminologies: 3D assets to design the appearance of light sources (like strip lights and lamps) and three light sources (directional, point and spotlight) to affect the ambient appearance of the scene and illuminate exhibits. Metaphoric connectors are used to link exhibition areas logically; for example, an elevator to connect levels of a building vertically and doors to connect rooms horizontally. Curators can place exhibits at absolute positions within an exhibition area or relative to (partition-)walls and assign camera poses for each exhibit and other points of interest. Furthermore, ViMCOX allows multilingual specification of exhibition areas, including descriptions and appellations; localization of visual elements in the 3D scene, like tooltips or the button panels of an elevator; language-specific object placement; and multilingual object and presentation metadata.

3 Digital Resources and Virtual Objects

ViMCOX uses a generic concept for storing multimedia objects (digital resources), virtual object instances (virtual objects), interaction patterns, and presentation metadata. Digital resources maintain a minimal set of rights management metadata and provide pointers to richer museum documentation or preservation metadata. Digital resources are used to specify multimedia objects with multiple representations, for instance, 3D models with different levels of detail, video files in different formats, or images in different resolutions. They keep track of the rights of the original work of art, their digital surrogates including divergent rights, or born digital art. These digital resources can be wrapped by virtual objects to apply properties for visualization purposes in the 3D scene, for example, a generic passe-partout or 2D/3D frame for paintings.

4 Interaction Pattern and Virtual Museum Tours

Different interaction patterns can be applied to virtual object instances using object references: **a**) combinable geometric modifications such as translation, rotation and scale, which allow visitors to view and examine exhibits from different vantage points; **b**) presentation behavior that defines how metadata, contextual information, and supplementary materials are accessed and presented; and **c**) navigation aids that bind predefined viewpoints for navigation purposes. While geometric interaction patterns are indicated as pictographs (HCI affordance) next to the exhibit, the interaction patterns **b** and **c** are mutually exclusive and applied directly to the exhibit. In addition to the presentation of metadata and supplementary material, ViMCOX facilitates the specification of virtual museum tours, which allow visitors to take part in guided and unguided tours offering a variety of multilingual supplementary materials. ViMCOX incorporates the TourML metadata scheme to define the contents, structure, and logic of a virtual museum tour.

5 Conclusion

ViMCOX addresses the standardization of the modeling of adaptive virtual museums with dynamically generated exhibition environments, fictional exhibition settings including digital surrogates or born digital objects, and reconstructions of physical exhibition space and museum architecture using 3D authoring software. In addition, ViMCOX provides stylistic devices for the modeling of virtual museum tours and the definition of presentation behavior to define how metadata and supplementary materials can be accessed by the visitor. Future research will address the development of tool sets to capture and evaluate user behavior in order to create adaptive virtual museums with cross-collection content and enriched user profiles with semantic recommendations.

References

1. Biella, D., Luther, W., and Baloian, N.: Beyond the ARCO Standard. 16th Inter- national Conference on Virtual Systems and Multimedia (VSMM), 184–191 (2010)
2. Biella, D., Luther, W:, and Sacher, D.: Schema Migration into a Web-based Framework for Generating Virtual Museums and Laboratories.18th International Conference on Virtual Systems and Multimedia (VSMM). IEEE, 307–314 (2012)
3. Sacher, D., Biella, D., and Luther, W.: A Generative Approach to Virtual Museums. 9th International Conference on Web Information Systems and Technologies (WEBIST 2013), Krempels K-H., and Stocker, A. (Eds.) SciTePress, 274–279 (2013)
4. Sacher, D. Biella, D., and Luther, W.: Towards a Versatile Metadata Exchange for- mat for Digital Museum Collections. Proceedings of the 2013 Digital Heritage International Congress (Digital Heritage), 129–136 (2013)
5. Wolf, V., Song, Y., Sacher, D., Luther, W., and Biella, D.: ViMCOX: Virtual Museum and Cultural Object Exchange Format, Specification Version 1.1

Virtual Museums
From Content Creation To Presentation

Daniel Sacher

University of Duisburg-Essen, Germany

SADUE13

Contents

Introduction
    ViMEDEAS
    Metadata in Cultural Heritage
    ViMCOX & Replicave

Exhibition Design
    Exhibition Templates
    ViMCOX
    Generative Virtual Museums
    Tour Design

Architecture

Summary

ViMEDEAS
Virtual Museum Exhibition Designer Using Enhanced ARCO
Standard (Curator Software) [1], [2], [3]

- ▶ Authoring tools and frameworks for webbased exhibitions
- ▶ Seeks to enhance design processes and supports user centered tasks

User groups

- ▶ Curators and content-creators
- ▶ (3D) Software developer
- ▶ Visitors, researcher, educators

Featureset

- ▶ Design, planning, archiving and dissemination
- ▶ Digitization and data acquisition
- ▶ Interaction design
- ▶ *Metadata administration and 3D visualization*

Metadata in Cultural Heritage

- Approx. 100 metadata standards available in the cultural heritage domain [4]
- Athena survey [5]
  - 130 institutions, 50 museums
  - Many in-house standards
  - Dublin Core is wide-spread and adopted
  - Organizations use appropriate formats and museum standards are not used by other domains

LIDO
Lightweight Information Describing Objects [6]

- Metadata harvesting and interchange format
  - Presentation and indexing
  - XML scheme based on international standards (Museumdat, CDWA Lite, Spectrum, CIDOC-CRM)
- Descriptive and administrative metadata
  - Multilingual
  - Cross-domain (fine-art, archeology, botany) at collection and item level
  - Supports controlled vocabulary and thesauri

ViMCOX
Virtual Museum and Cultural Object Exchange Format [7]

- Metadata set to describe virtual museums
- Adopts elements from existing metadata standards
  - Proposes extensions to cover missing concepts
    - Exhibition design and room arrangements
    - Illumination
    - Multimedia
    - Assets (windows, partition walls, furniture)
    - User centered aspects (navigation, interaction, dynamic objects, tours, POIs)
- Used as configuration for exhibition space generation

ViMCOX

Concept

- ► Common modeling language and specification
  - ► Free choice of authoring tools, graphic library, platform and OS
- ► Application driven visualization
- ► Abstract and declarative description of content
  - ► Maps to scenegraph concept
- ► Dynamic metadata-based generation of exhibitions, interior and room layout
  - ► Detached processes and tailored metadata

Replicave
3D content generation framework

- ► Technology: JavaSE 6+, JAXB, Servlet-Container - Tomcat 6+, X3D and X3Dom
- ► Exhibition templates and assets
- ► *Mapping of ViMCOX metadata elements*

Templates

- ► XML templates, multimedia CMS
- ► Room templates in rectangular or polyangular shape
- ► Exhibition templates (entrancehall, mediaroom, cloakroom, gallery)

ViMCOX Overview

- ► Interchange format conversion from Museumdat to LIDO v1.0
- ► Multilingualism
- ► New metadata elements and features
    - ► Simple user-object interaction (geometric modification, presentation, navigation aid)
    - ► Partition walls
    - ► Viewpoints (POIs)
    - ► Outdoor areas
    - ► Custom room shapes
    - ► 3D environmental models
    - ► Geometric windows and doors
    - ► Illumination
    - ► Tour design (TourML)

ViMCOX: Top Level

ViMCOX: Rooms

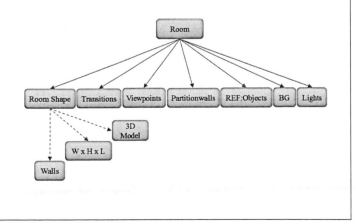

Digital Resources & Virtual Objects

Digital Resources (cf. CARARE [8])
Multimedia object documentation (3D, audio, video, images)

- ► Resource representation and measurements
- ► Rights of work, surrogates or born digital content
- ► Actors and roles
- ► Repository & record
- ► Pointer to external documentation (museum documentation, preservation, LOM, GML)

Virtual Objects

- ► Wrapper for Digital Resources
- ► Virtual attributes, e.g., Painting – generic passepartout and 2D/3D frame
- ► Positioning of multiple virtual object instances (absolute, relative to (partition-)walls)
- ► Addition of interaction patterns

Digital Resources, Virtual Objects & Interaction Pattern

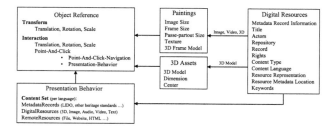

Figure : [9]

Multilingualism

- ► Multilingual object metadata, appellations and descriptions of stylistic devices as well as visual elements in the 3D scene
  - ► Tooltips, viewpoints, transitions, level names on elevator panels
  - ► Appellation and description of exhibition areas
  - ► Tour content and supplementary material
- ► xml:lang attributes instead of maintaining multiple language specific top level elements (cf. LIDO [6])

Lighting Component [9]

- Important task during exhibition design
- Light sources (3D models) and emitted light
- Abstract parameters defined based on OpenGL specification and equations
  - Directional-, Point-, SpotLight

Lighting Component – Limitations

- PerPixel vs. PerVertex Lighting
- Deferred Shading for more than 8 active hardware lights
- Requires WYSIWYG-Editor

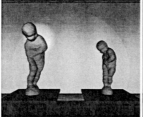

Figure : [9]

Exhibition space

- Rectangular
- Custom shapes with arbitrary wall positioning
  - Topologic maps and 2D floorplans
  - Geometric windows, doors and passages using parameters
- Partition walls
- Metaphoric connectors (teleporter, door, elevator)

Figure : [3]

Figure : [3]

Exhibition space appearance and texturing

- ▶ No UV-mapping but texture wrapping (floor, ceiling, walls)
- ▶ Limitation: light maps, bump maps and shading not part of ViMCOX
- ▶ No modeling of room's exterior
- ▶ *Therefore support for 3D models as exhibition space*

Interaction

- ▶ Geometric modification & reversibility [3]
- ▶ Translation, rotation, scale
- ▶ Combined interaction
- ▶ Affordances (HCI)
- ▶ Automatic and custom parametrization in Replicave

Point & Click Navigation [9]

- ▶ Navigation 'LookAt' for touch screens, binds predefined viewpoint
- ▶ Specify transition types (interpolation, teleport, collision free path)

Interaction: Presentation Behavior [9]

Museum documentation
Plain museum documentation not suitable for heterogeneous audiences [10]

- ▶ Put objects into context
- ▶ Link related information and supplementary material
- ▶ Tailor information based on user groups
- ▶ Provide different presentation styles

Disadvantages 3D visualization
Visual quality affected by viewing angle, distance and low-resolution models or textures.

Interaction

Presentation Behavior
Define how contextual information are accessed and presented

- ▶ Access: information cards or plagues, image maps using 2D/3D geometry
- ▶ Visualization: 2D overlay, frameset, HUD, HTML markup
- ▶ View-Template: gallery, slideshow, mediaplayer, external application

Figure : [9]

Presentation Behavior – ContentSet (per language)

Metadata Resources

- ▶ Pointer to museum documentation metadata file
- ▶ Qualified metadata expressed in payload, e.g., GML Point

Digital Resources

- ▶ Audio, video, image, 3D
- ▶ PropertySet: caption, playback, size ...

Remote Resources
External resources: files, websites, HTML, PDF ...

Generative Approach [11]

- ▶ Algorithmic floor planning, e.g., 2D pointlist, object distribution, curves, TreeMaps, ShapeGrammar, graph dualization, Solr-Query ...
- ▶ Fast prototyping, re-use and re-arrangement of rooms
- ▶ Efficient with large content bases and when regular polygonal room shapes are desired
- ▶ May require manual post-processing

The Virtual Leopold Fleischhacker Museum [12]

- ► On display are 200 photographs and 30 3D models
- ► Conceptual layout was drafted into ground plot sketches
  - ► Asset and object positions
  - ► Room arrangements and layout
- ► Thematic exhibitions across 13 exhibition rooms and one outdoor area

Parameter Design

- ► Abstraction of ground plot sketches and simplified parameter design
  - ► Ordered list of objects and transitions per wall
  - ► Additional object parameters for room construction
  - ► Virtual object dimensions are stored in ViMCOX object instances
- ► Algorithm calculates room dimensions, object positions, transitions, viewpoints, texture wrapping and interaction modes

Post-processing

- ► Assignment of suitable textures and color coordination
- ► Fine-tuning of object positions and scale
- ► Addition of picture frames or passepartouts
- ► Inclusion of assets, plants, furniture or avatars

Tour Design [13], [14]

Tour Stops
Tour Stops as Viewpoints

- ► Marking Points Of Interest (POIs)
- ► Architectural parts that are not explicitly defined as exhibit (frescos)

Tour Logic
State automaton – 1 stop active at a time

- ► Connections as directed graphs to specify tour sequences
- ► Conditions and constraints

Tour Design

Tour Conditions
Free and guided tours using Activation and Deactivation Events
- ▶ Spatial proximity (BBOX, DISTANCE)
- ▶ Mouse event (CLICK)
- ▶ Duration of visit

Tour Content
Defined similar to the Presentation Behavior
- ▶ Specification of multilingual supplementary material, appellations, descriptions and properties
- ▶ View-Templates
- ▶ Link exhibition areas

Tour ML

Tour ML
Maintained by Indianapolis Museum of Art, developed in a community process by domain experts and museum staff [15]
- ▶ XML schema to store tour structure and content
- ▶ Application driven visualization and tour logic implementation
- ▶ Media assets and rights, tour stops, connections as graph

Application specific properties
- ▶ Linked Exhibition Area: ID
- ▶ Viewpoint: ID or disjoint viewpoint
- ▶ Set of Activation/Deactivation Events
  - ▶ PROXIMITY#objX#5.0
  - ▶ DURATION#120
- ▶ Other relevant properties: transition type, ...

VM Tour: Studentproject

Figure : [9]

Schema migration

- Merging of Replicave's and ViMCOX' feature sets
- 3 tier architecture
- Generative approach and metadata-based modelling
  - Detached processes
  - Programmatic and procedural generation of exhibit space
  - Eased maintenance and refactoring

Schema mapping

Figure : [3]

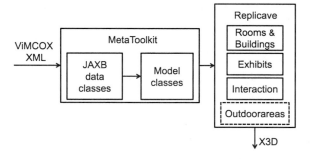

Architecture: user groups and workflow

Figure : [3]

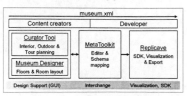

Architecture: workspace, dissemination, rendering

Figure : [11]

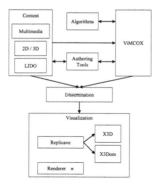

Summary

Addressed Topics

- ▸ Architectural design and exhibit arrangement
  - ▸ Reconstructions and fictional exhibitions
- ▸ Presentation of museum documentation or context-oriented and didactically enhanced material
- ▸ Tour content and supplementary material
- ▸ Linked data and cross-collection content (OAI-PMH)
  - ▸ YCBA, Rijksmuseum
  - ▸ Apache Solr server

Goal: Adaptive Virtual Museums

- ▸ User-Profiles, capture and evaluate behavior, semantic recommendations
- ▸ Handheld indoor-localization

Acknowledgment

Many thanks to our project partners from the Salomon Ludwig Steinheim-Institut and our students Henrik Detjen, Marco Janc, Simon Leßmann, Dominic Ripkens, Sabine Steffen, Markus Stolzenburg, Lukas Stukenbrock and Serdar Yaslar for their valuable summaries; careful implementation of the software; provision of 3D models, textures and screenshots; and building The Virtual Leopold Fleischhacker Museum.

References I

- D. Biella, W. Luther, and N. Baloian, "Beyond the ARCO standard," in *16th International Conference on Virtual Systems and Multimedia (VSMM)*, 2010, pp. 184–191.

- D. Biella, W. Luther, and N. Baloian, "Virtual Museum Exhibition Designer Using Enhanced ARCO Standard," in *XXIX International Conference of the Chilean Computer Science Society (SCCC)*, November 2010, pp. 226–235.

- D. Biella, W. Luther, and D. Sacher, "Schema migration into a web-based framework for generating virtual museums and laboratories," in *18th International Conference on Virtual Systems and Multimedia (VSMM)*. IEEE, 2012, pp. 307–314.

- D. Becker and J. Riley, "Seeing standards: A visualization of the metadata universe," in *7th Iteration (2011): Science Maps as Visual Interfaces to Digital Libraries*, 2010. [Online]. Available: http://scimaps.org/

References II

- G. McKenna and C. De Loof, "Athena d3.1 report on existing standards applied by european museums," 2010, [Online; accessed 05.11.2012]. [Online]. Available: http://www.athenaeurope.org/getFile.php?id=396

- E. Coburn, R. Light, G. Mckenna, R. Stein, and A. Vitzthum. (2010) LIDO: Lightweight Information Describing Objects, Specification Version 1.0. [Online]. Available: http://www.lido-schema.org/schema/v1.0/lido-v1.0-specification.pdf

- V. Wolf, Y. Song, D. Sacher, W. Luther, and D. Biella. (2012) ViMCOX: Virtual Museum and Cultural Object Exchange Format, Specification Version 1.1. [Online]. Available: http://www.vimedeas.com/wordpress/?page_id=40

References III

- CARARE. (2013) CARARE metadata schema outline v1.1. [Online]. Available: http://www.carare.eu/eng/content/download/4277/35150/file/CARARE%20metadata%20schema%20outline%20v1.1.pdf

- D. Sacher, D. Biella, and W. Luther, "Towards a versatile metadata exchange format for digital museum collections," 2013, accepted at Digital Heritage 2013 conference.

- W. Schweibenz, "How to create the worst online exhibition possible - in the best of intention," *Museumskunde, Band 76, 1/2011, S.90-99*, 2012.

- D. Sacher, D. Biella, and W. Luther, "A generative approach to virtual museums," in *WEBIST 2013 - Proceedings of the 9th International Conference on Web Information Systems and Technologies*, 2013.

References IV

D. Sacher, M. Brocke, M. Heitmann, B. Kaufhold, W. Luther, and D. Biella, "The Virtual Leopold Fleischhacker Museum," in *Museums and the Web 2013: Proceedings*, 2013.

L. Chittaro, L. Ieronutti, R. Ranon, E. Siotto, and D. Visintini, "A high-level tool for curators of 3D virtual visits and ist application to a virtual exhibition of renaissance frescoes," in *Proceedings of the 11th International conference on Virtual Reality, Archaeology and Cultural Heritage.* Eurographics Association, 2010, pp. 147–154.

L. Chittaro, L. Ieronutti, and R. Ranon, "VEX-CMS: A tool to design virtual exhibitions and walkthroughs that integrates automatic camera control capabilities," in *Smart Graphics.* Springer, 2010, pp. 103–114.

References V

R. Stein and N. Proctor, "TourML: An Emerging Specification for Museum Mobile Experiences," in *Museums and the Web 2011: Proceedings*, 2011.

Challenges and Chances

Song Liu
North China Electric Power University
liusong@ncepu.edu.cn

In April 2013, I changed my workplace from Waseda University in Japan to the North China Electric Power University (NCEPU) in China. There, I created a new institute called the Institute of Intelligent Grid Technology and was selected as the director of this institute. Since the research and education environment is different in China than in Japan, I have faced many challenges—and many new opportunities.

1 Introduction to NCEPU

Fig. 1. Official Web page and location of NCEPU

The North China Electric Power University (NCEPU) is affiliated with the Ministry of Education and is officially listed as one of the 211 Project and 985 Project universities as well as a Predominant Discipline Innovation Platform. It comprises two campuses—one in Beijing and one in Baoding, with its main campus in northwest Beijing. The university was founded in 1958. The campus covers an area of over 1 million square meters. At present, the university has more than 27,000 full-time students, including more than 6,800 postgraduates, and its teaching staff totals 1,760 professional teachers, including 347 professors. The university maintains 62 bachelor's programs, 52 master's programs, 20 Ph.D. programs, and 4 mobile stations of post-doctoral scientific research. For many years, NCEPU graduates have enjoyed an employment rate of over 96%.

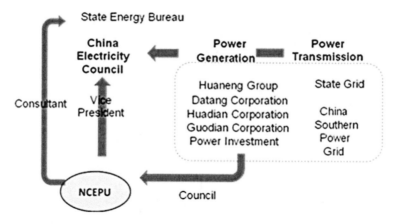

Fig. 2. Position of NCEPU in the Chinese power industry

At present, NCEPU is a key university jointly constructed by the Ministry of Education and the University Council, which is composed of State Grid Corporation of China, China Southern Power Grid Co., Ltd., China Huaneng Group, China Datang Corporation, China Huadian Corporation, China Guodian Corporation and China Power Investment Corporation.

2 New Challenges and Opportunities

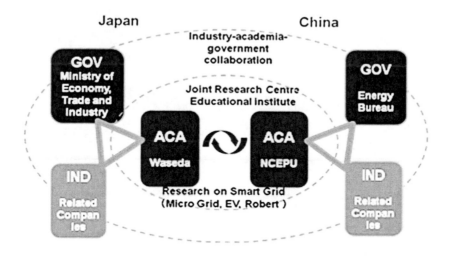

Fig. 3. Cooperation between Waseda University and NCEPU

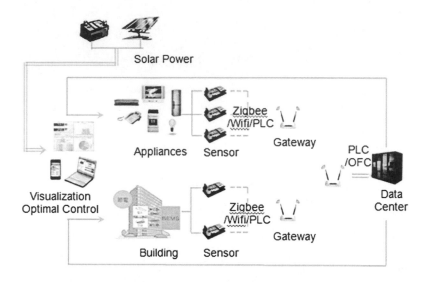

Fig. 4. BEMS (Building Energy Management System) project

We are currently organizing a cooperation between Waseda University and NCEPU to perform joint research on smart grids, especially on microgrids for electric vehicles. We are planning to create a joint research center and educational institute with the collaboration of industry, academia, and government in both countries.

As an example of this cooperation, one project we have proposed is the Building Energy Management System (BEMS). This project will comprise the following steps:

- Step1. Develop an energy management system (EMS) to implement electric power usage visualization.
- Step2. Implement the EMS in buildings and gather electric power usage data, combined with other data—how many people work in an office, what hours they work, weather data, and so forth—to analyze power usage patterns. Conduct contrast experiments with other buildings to deduce an optimized power control plan.
- Step3. Add a solar power system and generate a new optimized power control plan.

Challenges and Chances

North China Electric Power University
Song Liu

Location

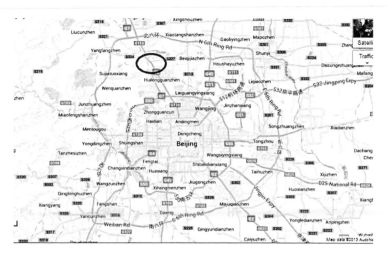

Power Industry in China

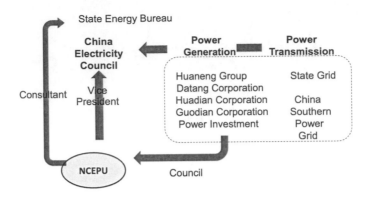

School and Department

1. Electrical & Electronic Engineering School
2. Energy & Power Engineering School
3. Renewable Energy School
4. Nuclear Science & Engineering School
5. BusinessAdministration School
6. ComputerScience & Technology School
7. ControlScience & Engineering School
8. EnvironmentEngineering & Science School
9. Human & Social Science School
10. Mathematical & Physical Science School
11. Foreign Language School
12. Science & Technology School

Waseda & NCEPU

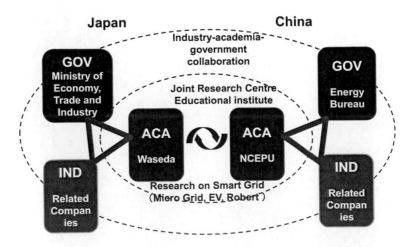

BEMS(Building Energy Management System)

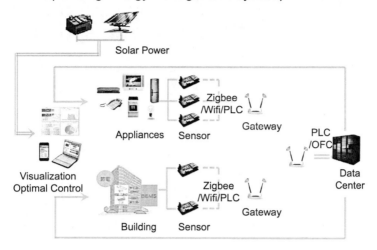

Thank you very much & Welcome to Beijing!

Song Liu
liusong@ncepu.edu.cn
skype: liusong

Reliable Computing in Modeling and Simulating Software

Recent contributions by the Computer Graphics and Scientific
Computing Group at UDE

Wolfram Luther
Department of Computer Science and Applied Cognitive Sciences
University of Duisburg-Essen
luther@inf.uni-due.de

The purpose of this presentation is to provide an overview of the SADUE13 workshop, which was recently organized by the Department of Computer Science (DCC) at the University of Chile (Prof. Nelson Baloian) and the Department of Computer Science and Applied Cognitive Science at the University of Duisburg-Essen (Prof. Wolfram Luther). The workshop continues collaboration that was established during the tri-national PhD academies SADUEWA 2008, 2009, and 2010 together with the University of Waseda (Prof. Yoshiyori Urano). This collaboration focuses on semantic technologies for interactive and learning support systems, integrating mobile and ubiquitous computing components, knowledge management and decision-making systems, and analytical information systems that assist users in performing various analyses, such as traffic simulation systems, security, and assistance. Some of the specific topics treated were the evaluation of CSCW systems from several viewpoints, ambient assisted living applications, user interface adaptation and recommendation based on external context factors, and user models and interaction context.

The main goal of the meeting was to take an initial step towards establishing a network of young researchers in the field of ambient intelligence in metropolitan regions focusing on ubiquitous, context-aware, distributed, and reliable computing and bringing together people from the Rhine-Ruhr region in Germany, Santiago in Chile, and the Beijing region in China. The workshop was funded by the DFG, the DAAD, and the CONICYT.

One of the intended results of the cooperation within the network is a new concept of cooperative publication of scientific results: a prototypical open access publication including rich and interactive content over a three-year period accompanied by several workshops.

The SADUE13 workshop is also a state of the art event, bringing together young professors, their teachers, and their PhD candidates to deepen fruitful cooperation activities, highlight new research questions, and prepare common publications.

The participants want to express their gratitude to the DFG for funding the meeting and the publication of the material presented during the last week of August 2013. For this publication, the presentation slides have been augmented by short introductions.

The following presentation is entitled "Reliable Computing in Modeling and Simulating Software" and provides an overview on new software tools worked out in projects funded by the DFG and the EU Ziel 2 program [10, 12] with special emphasis on accurate results even under uncertainty in the model parameters.

These systems have a strong link to the workshop theme even if they did not explicitly include a sensor network that collects data to build a part of the real world, reconstruct or classify objects, detect subjects' activities or users' intentions, or try to support users in activities like finding information, completing a task, or optimizing a solution. A framework that applies ambient intelligence in such ways as synchronizing applications with users' mobile devices or supporting them in their daily lives must take into account uncertainty in parameters and guarantee accuracy in the outcome of algorithms. This can be achieved via validation metrics that help to compute a degree of similarity or to compare reconstructed objects and their behavior with their real world instances.

In our recent research, we identified various forms in which uncertainty arises:

In two projects MOBILEBODY and PROREOP, a consortium of engineers, IT researchers, and medical scientists developed and evaluated new tools for training, planning, and assessing total hip replacements (THR). The general aim of a THR surgery is to align the implant so that the fitness with the femoral stem is maximized. A fitness measure can be defined by the distance between the relevant areas of the implant and the surface of the medullary space which receives the implant, (e.g., smaller than 2 mm in a cementless THR).

The segmentation process can produce trochanter major images with a systematic input data error of $1.5 - 2$ mm or $2°$, respectively, which considerably impacts geometric features such as femur length or orientation [6]. However, we showed in [2, 4] that the model error for the distance between a point on the surface and the multicomponent model of the prosthesis was at most 10^{-2}mm. This means that the error in the position is influenced mainly by the uncertainty in the data acquisition by MRI and CT imagery as well as by bone and muscle segmentation—and not by the uncertainty caused by the distance algorithm, which belongs to class 1 of our *Numerical Verification and Validation Taxonomy* [1], which extends work done by Oberkampf et al. [9]. A computer-based system model belongs to this class if and only if uncertainty is quantified and propagated throughout the system using verified or stochastic approaches, or both. All computations are executed using tools and algorithms with result verification. Alternatively, real number algorithms, analytical solutions, or computer-aided existence proofs are used. Software and hardware comply with IEEE754 and follow the interval standard P1788 actually under final discussion.

Handling and propagating both uncertainty and numerical errors through complex computations is fully supported in Stefan Kiel's UniVerMeC, a framework for the development, assessment, and interoperable use of verified techniques [3, 4], which provides different interval arithmetics, uniform function representation, and interfaces to powerful numerical algorithms with result verification.

A completely different form of uncertainty appears in historical texts with nonstandard spelling. In [5] we present a rule-based fuzzy search engine that allows users to retrieve text data independently of its orthographical realization in texts edited several hundred years before the German spelling reform of 1901. This search engine allows users to find terms in an old text by inputting the modern spelling even if there are a multitude of corresponding historical spellings depending on the date or region of origin and the text genre. Thus, a single object has a multiset of instances that is not completely known. We intentionally did not focus on the use of a dictionary since it can efficiently index only a fraction of the possible variants.

Two recent approaches have addressed this issue. One is rule-based transformations, which generate possible spellings with rules generated and validated or selected on the fly; this leads to a slim, flexible, and ultimately highly sustainable tool. The other is a Java framework for fuzzy full-text retrieval on nonstandard texts based on letter replacement rules as well as trained string edit distances; it was developed in Thomas Pilz's PhD thesis and also exists as an easy-to-use plugin that works with current Web browsers.

A further application deals with verified parameter estimation in stochastic traffic modeling. Here, uncertainty means that transmission time and volume are usually unknown and unpredictable when transmission demands are created by the users and applications. In several funded projects carried out in collaboration with Dr. Haßlinger and Deutsche Telekom [7], we have proposed algorithms to accurately compute the verified stationary workload distributions of GI/GI/1 and SMP/GI/1 service systems using factorization approaches and subsequently the transient behavior of the queue and the time required for the system to reach equilibrium.

In conclusion, we are confident that today uncertainty and accuracy issues should and will be addressed in the design phase of any computer-based modeling and simulation system.

1 Verification & Validation (V&V) assessment

- Introduction
- V &V assessment: Modeling, simulation and validation cycle for femur endo-prosthesis
- Workflow in exemplary modeling and simulation (M&S) process
- Tool support
- Blockwise fitting to V&V class hierarchy
- Proposal for classification and standardization

2 Modeling/Simulation vs V&V

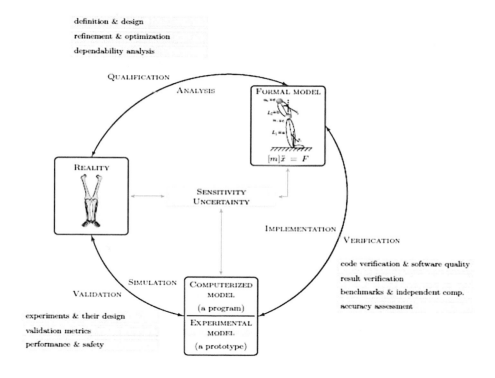

Figure 1: Verification and validation cycle

Schlesinger, S. [11]; Auer, Cuypers, Luther [4]

3 Some definitions and insights

Verification: The process of determining that a model implementation accurately represents the developer's conceptual description of the model and the solution to the model.
Validation: The process of determining the degree to which a model is an accurate representation of the real world from the perspective of its intended uses.

Validation must assess the predictive capability of the model in the specific realm of interest and address uncertainties that arise from both simulation results and experimental data [8].

4 PO Verification Guidelines: Goals

I Workflow description

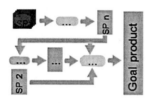

Requirements

- Software functionalities
- Parallelization/realtime require-ments
- Exchange formats, data transfer
- Documentation and customization

↓

II Computational & formal models
    Definition, system classification, action logic

↓

III Verification extent and congruence assessment
    Verification degree, verification tools, interoperability

↓

IV User support
    Recommenders, comparison systems, result reporting

5 Numerical V&V Assessment

Questionnaires: Input data, models, data types, functions/algorithms, output (data)
Verification degree:

Class 4: Purely floating or fixed-point implementation
Class 3: Standardized floating point arithmetics with uncertainty management, error bounds or self-correcting algorithms

Class 2: Verification of relevant subsystems, tools with result verification, computer-aided proofs

Class 1: Purely verified implementation

6 V&V Assessment Domains

- Computational physics
- Geostatistics: Modeling spatial uncertainty
- Economics
- Stability analysis of continuous-time control systems with bounded parameter uncertainties
- Water resources research
- Weather and forecasting
- Software quality assurance practices
- Statistical software engineering
- …..

7 Types of Uncertainty

- *Experimental (Aleatory) uncertainty (EU)* - uncertainty in the parameters of interest
  o Methods for overcoming EU: Monte Carlo, Fuzzy logic, interval uncertainty, ….
- *Epistemic uncertainty* (model form uncertainty)
  o Insufficient experimental base (foundation)
  o Limited understanding of complex physical processes
  o Insufficient knowledge concerning initial conditions and boundary conditions
- It is necessary to manage the uncertainties.

8 Ways to Achieve Accuracy / Reliability Classification

- Uncertainty quantification
- Accuracy assessment
- Tools with result verification
- Sensitivity analysis
- A priori / a posteriori error bounds
- Independent computations
- Performance analysis
- Benchmark examples and standardized test tools

9 Verification Software

- Tools and verified versions
    - C++ → C-XSC (Krämer)
    - MATLAB® → INTLAB (Rump)
    - IPP → DSI (Limbourg, Rebner)
    - Global optimization solvers
    - Modeling software: MOBILE (Kecskeméthy) → SmartMOBILE (Auer)
- Analyzing numerical precision
    - Cadna++ (Lamotte et al.), Fluctuat (CEA)
- Creating interfaces between various tools
    - C-XSC, MATLAB®, RiskCalc Plus™, ….
- VERICOMP: A system for comparing and assessing verified IVP solvers (E. Auer, A. Rauh)
- UniVerMeC: A framework for interoperable use of verified techniques (St. Kiel)

10 Application Context

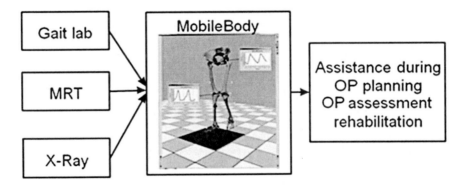

Figure 2: Project workflow

Chief coordination: Prof. A. Kecskeméthy (UDE)

Our tasks: Accurate hip prosthesis fitting, characterization of uncertainty

11 Modeling and Simulation Processes in Detail

- Dynamic gait simulation under uncertainty in parameters (E. Auer)
- Geometrical contact and intersection testing: Modeling foot contact (A. Kecskeméthy)
- Superquadric (SQ) bone and prosthesis modeling (R. Cuypers, 2011 [6])
- Bone prosthesis fitting into the medullary space of the routed femoral shaft: Total hip arthroplasty (THA) (R. Cuypers, 2011)

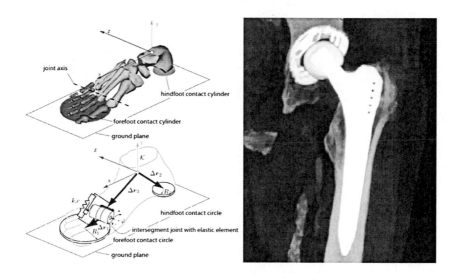

12 Insertion Process

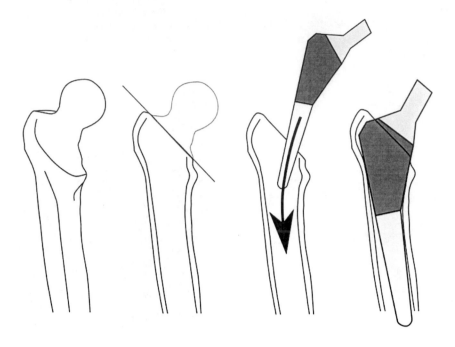

13 Total Hip Arthroplasty: Workflow

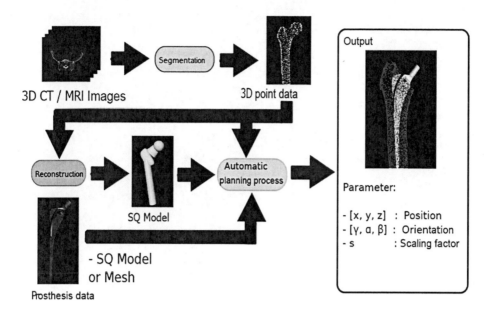

14 Verification and Validation Hardware and Software Blocks

- Description: XML, UML
- Data acquisition (Pre-selection: MRI device, CT) (F. Löer)
- Accuracy: Dependent on the resolution of the MRI and its signal-to-noise ratio
- Segmentation (J. Pauli, Z. Tang)
- Superquadrics modeling and fitting (R. Cuypers)
  - Distance between convex SQs, Optimization, K-segments algorithms
  - Parameters: $a_1, a_2, a_3 \geq \tau$, $\varepsilon_1, \varepsilon_2 \in [\tau, 2 - \tau]$, where τ is a positive safety parameter
  - Feature extraction (R. Cuypers, S. Ladd)
  - Verified distance computation (A. Chuev, St. Kiel)
- Pose computation (R. Cuypers)
- Representation: The world coordinate system of the MRI scan data $\Rightarrow$ Virtual reality prognosis and diagnosis system

15 SQ Modeling

$$F(x,y,z) = \left(\left(\frac{x}{a_1} \right)^{\frac{2}{\varepsilon_2}} + \left(\frac{y}{a_2} \right)^{\frac{2}{\varepsilon_2}} \right)^{\frac{\varepsilon_2}{\varepsilon_1}} + \left(\frac{z}{a_3} \right)^{\frac{2}{\varepsilon_1}} = 1$$

$\varepsilon_2 = 0$

$\varepsilon_2 = 1$

$\varepsilon_2 = 2$

$\varepsilon_1 = 0$ $\varepsilon_1 = 1$ $\varepsilon_1 = 2$

Class 1: Algorithms and operations
- Point in/on/out of SQ
- Derivative, normal, point to given normal
- Distance between convex SQs using support mapping function (A. Chuev)
  - Verified result obtained by GJK algorithm a posteriori
- Distance between generalized SQs using the hierarchical decomposition approach
  - Unified Framework for Verified GeoMetric Computations (S. Kiel)

Class 2: Feature extraction
Uncertainty in features is caused by errors in the input data and not by the distance algorithm! (1.5 mm vs. 10^{-4} mm)

Class 3: MRI/CT, segmentation, K-segments, NAG optimization

16 Use of K-Segments Algorithm

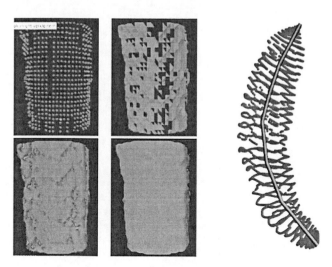

Figure 3: Surface mesh model of femur cavity - bended superquadric model

17 Generalized SQ Fitting

$$E(S) = \sqrt{a_1 a_2 a_3} \sum_{i=1}^{N} (F_S^{\varepsilon_1}(x_i, y_i, z_i) - 1)^2 \qquad \text{Class 3}$$

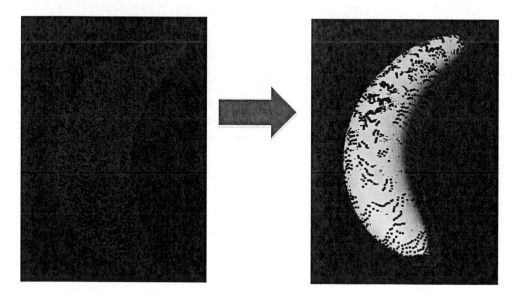

18 THR Requirements

- Minimization of the distance between the mechanically relevant areas of the implant and the medullary space
- Maximization of implant component size without exceeding the space given by the uncovered medullary space opening
- Maximal scaling (PressFit)
- Preservation of the individual bone features
- Supplier's requirements

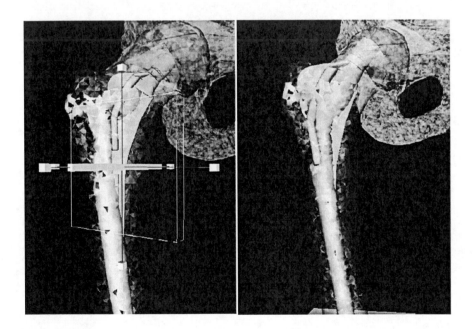

Figure 4: THR simulation: Insertion and iterated repositioning (Cuypers, 2011 [6])

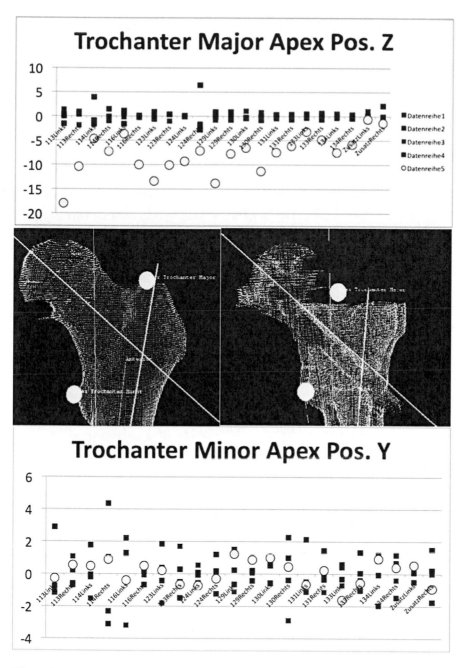

Figure 5: Measured (blue) and simulated parameter values using segmentation (with systematic error for Trochanter Major) (Cuypers 2011 [6])

19 Unified Framework for Verified GeoMetric Computations
S. Kiel UniVerMeC

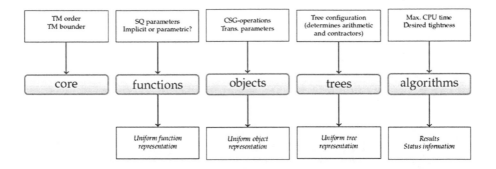

Figure 6: User input and corresponding output at the different abstraction levels of UniVerMeC for the distance computation use case

20 Vericomp Framework

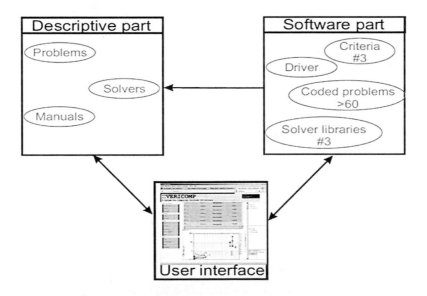

Figure 7: User support: Comparison of IVP solvers (Auer, Rauh 2011 [3])

21 General Problem Definition und Classification

(<u>Nonstiff</u>) Initial value problems of the form:

$$x^{\cdot}(t) = f(x(t)) \, , \ x(t_0) \in [\, x^0], $$

- $t_0 = 0, \, t \in [0; \, t_f] \subset \mathbf{R}$ for some $t_f > 0$
- $[x^0] = [\underline{x}^0 ; \overline{x}^0]$
- f can depend on parameters p with $[p] = [\underline{p} ; \overline{p}]$
- The problem is discretized
- The solution is $[x_{\underline{k}}]$ with $x(t_{\underline{k}} ; 0, [x_0]) \subseteq [x_{\underline{k}}]$

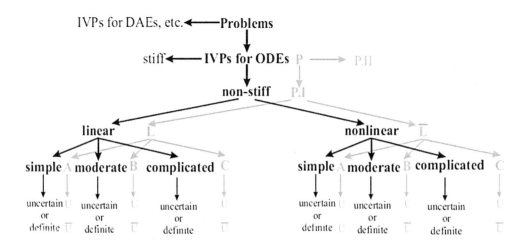

22 Criteria

C1 Number of arithmetic operations in a time step
C2 Number of function/Jacobian, etc./inverse matrix evaluations
C3 Overhead
C4 Wall clock time
C5 User CPU time wrt. overestimation
C6 Time to break-down t_{bd} for each solver
C7 Total number of steps and number of accepted steps.

Each criterion can be weighted to correspond to the application

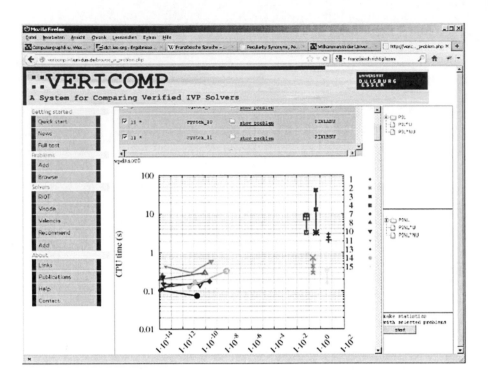

Figure 8: Vericomp user interface (http://vericomp.inf.uni-due.de/)

Example:

Solvers with specific parameters

ValEncIA 0.025, 0.0025, 0.00025

VNODE-LP 10, 15, 20

RiOT 5, 10, 15

Goal: To justify the classification

Means: WPD (Work precision diagrams)

23 Personalized Fuzzy Search in Historical Texts with Non-standard Spelling (C. Buck, T. Pilz, K. Dubovizky, W. Luther)

- Full text searches are important in almost all areas of literary science.
- Nontrivial search services are still marginal or even nonexistent.

- The few applications with standard edit distance metrics fail as soon as historical spellings appear in texts.
- Our proposal: Fuzzy search framework for historical texts

24 Starting Point

- Given: Text - Pattern
- Retrieve all segments of the text with an **edit distance ≤ k**
- Edit distance e *is the minimum number of* character insertions, deletions, or substitutions to make them equal → **Levenshtein distance**
- Example: Distance between s=Hercules and t=Heracles
- Edit distance between s and t is $D_{s,t} = 2$
- Hercules → Heraules (substitution of 'c' for 'a')
- Heraules → Heracles (substitution of 'u' for 'c')

25 FlexMetric

- Tables are calculated from word pairs of standard and historical spellings
- Currently several tables are trained on 13,000 word pairs

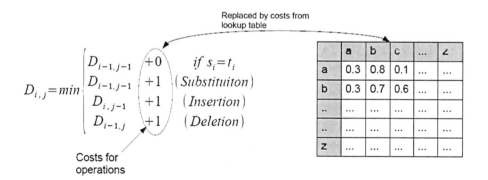

Replaced by costs from lookup table

$$D_{i,j} = min \begin{cases} D_{i-1,j-1} & +0 & if\ s_i = t_i \\ D_{i-1,j-1} & +1 & (Substituiton) \\ D_{i,j-1} & +1 & (Insertion) \\ D_{i-1,j} & +1 & (Deletion) \end{cases}$$

Costs for operations

	a	b	c	...	z
a	0.3	0.8	0.1	...	...
b	0.3	0.7	0.6	...	...
..	...	...	...	...	...
..	...	...	...	...	...
z	...	...	...	...	...

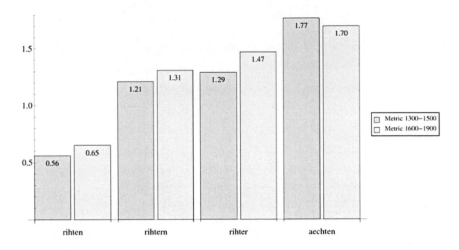

Figure 9: Example: *richten* in *Bayrischer Landfrieden* (1292)

26 WebMetric

- Uses Flexmetric for fuzzy search
  - User chooses adequate metric for the text
  - Algorithm calculates distance between search word and every word in the text
- Outcome:
  - List sorted by distance
  - Words are highlighted according to their distance

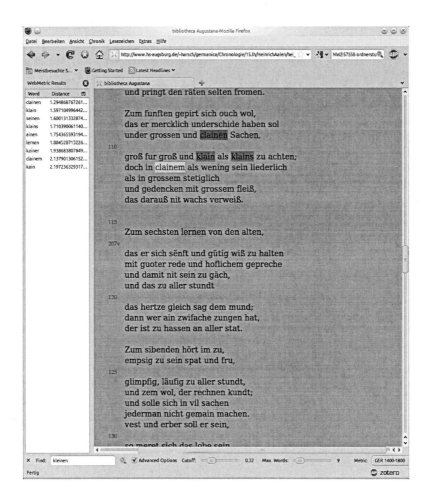

Figure 10: Search results for "Find: kleinen"

27 Project Proposal ValidRoute (with G. Haßlinger, Telekom 2009)

- Simulation of discrete stochastic systems: Transient analysis
- Searching and routing in networks with partial target information
- Storage of huge data measuring moving objects over a long time interval
  (spatial-temporal data reduction)
- Accurate interpolation of trajectories after strong compression in time
- Construction of inner and outer enclosures for time and place of moving
  objects
  Development of interval-based query languages
- Defining and updating group membership for mobile objects depending on
  various criteria

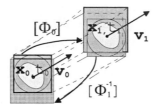

$$\mathbf{x}(t) = \Phi_i(\mathbf{x}_i, \mathbf{p}_i, t) = \mathbf{x}_i + \mathbf{v}_i t + \mathbf{b}_t \cdot t^2/2$$
$$[\Phi_0]([\mathbf{x}_0], \mathbf{p}_0, [t]) = [[\mathbf{x}_0] + [\mathbf{v}_0][t] + [\mathbf{b}][t]^2/2]$$

Figure 11: Parabolic truncated pyramid as forward and backward enclosures of uncertain object trajectories

28 Verdikom (with G. Haßlinger, Deutsche Telekom)

- Modeling
  - Modeling of original data traffic sources with semi–Markov models: Assigning values of given trace to particular states with a variety of methods (deterministic, genetic optimization) with good representation of autocorrelation
  - Aggregation of several sources: Superposition of SMPs
  - Combine with models of service capacity to SMP/G/1 queuing system

- Analysis
  - Verified polynomial factorization: Workload distribution
  - Verified Wiener-Hopf factorization: Workload distribution, idle and busy times

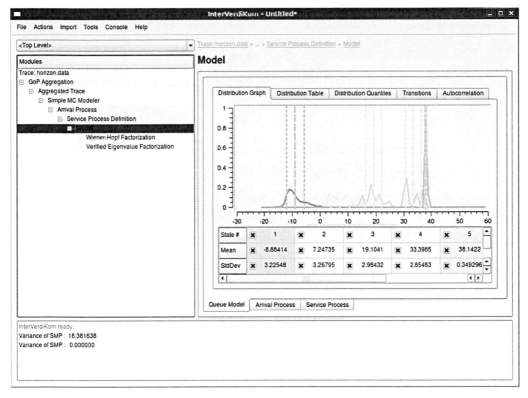

Figure 12: InterVerdiKom user interface (S. Kempken 2009 [8])

29 Conclusions

- Various occurrences of uncertainty in the process modeling and simulation workflow
- Challenges
- Various modeling approaches
- Reduction of complexity
- Task model needed: Requirements
- Wide spectrum of data structures and algorithms involved
- Computational issues: Performance, reliability, RTC
- Appropriate metrics allow measuring of similarities between mental or computer-based models and real process
- Verification and validation assessment required

30 Acknowledgements

Thanks to

Dr. Ph. Limbourg, Dr. E. Auer, Dr. Dyllong, Dr. S. Kempken, S. Kiel, Dr. T. Pilz, G. Rebner, D. Sacher, Dr. B. Weyers and Dr. R. Cuypers for their contributions,

to our partners Dr. Haßlinger (Deutsche Telekom), Dr. Rauh (Rostock), Profs. Baloian, Pino, Ochoa, Weber (UChile)

Profs. Ammon, Kecskeméthy, Kluge, Söffker (UDE)

Profs. R. Alt (UMC Paris), M. Beer (Liverpool), E. Walter, M. Kieffer Supélec , V. Kreinovich (El Paso), N. Stewart (Montreal)

and to the DAAD, DFG and Ziel 2 program (EU) for funding this work.

References

1. Auer, E., and Luther, W.: Numerical verification assessment in computational biomechanics. In A. Cuyt, W. Krämer, W. Luther, and P. Markstein, editors, Numerical Validation in Current Hardware Architectures, Lecture Notes in Computer Science 5492, Springer, 145–160 (2009)
2. Auer, E., Chuev, A., Cuypers, R., Kiel, S., and Luther, W.: Relevance of Accurate and Verified Numerical Algorithms for Verification and Validation in Biomechanics. In Euromech Colloqium 511: Biomechanics of Human Motion Proceedings, March 2011.
3. Auer, E., Rauh, A.: VERICOMP: A system to compare and assess verified IVP solvers. Computing 94 (2-4), 163–172 (2011). DOI 10.1007/10.1007/s00607-011-0178-4
4. Auer, E., Cuypers, R., and Luther, W.: Process-oriented Approach to Verification in Biomechanics, 11th Int. Conf. on Structural Safety & Reliability, in Safety, Reliability, Risk and Life-Cycle Performance of Structures and Infrastructures by George Deodatis, Bruce R. Ellingwood , Dan M. Frangopol (eds.). Taylor Francis 391-398 (2013)
5. Buck, C., Pilz, T., W. Luther, W.: Personalized Fuzzy Search in Historical Texts with Nonstandard Spelling. Linguistic Studies of Human Language (G. Rata Ed.), ATINER Athens, 325–336 (2013)
6. Cuypers, R.: Geometrische Modellierung mit Superquadriken zur Optimierung skeletaler Diagnosesysteme, PhD Thesis, Duisburg 2011 (in German), Logos (2011)
7. Kempken, S., Hasslinger, G., and Luther, W.: Parameter estimation and optimization techniques for discrete-time semi-Markov models of H.264/AVC video traffic. Telecommunication Systems, Springer (2008)
8. Kempken, S.: Modellierung und verifizierte Analyse von zeitkorreliertem Datenverkehr im Internet. Dissertation, Universität Duisburg-Essen. VDI Verlag, Düsseldorf, Informatik/Kommunikation Series, No. 804 (2009) ISBN 978-3-18-380410-8
9. Oberkampf, W. L., Trucano, T. G., and Hirsch, C.: Verification, Validation, and Predictive Capability in Computational Engineering and Physics. SAND2003-3769, Sandia National Laboratories (2003)

10. Rauh, A., Auer, E., Hofer, E.P., and Luther, W. (Eds.): Verified Methods: Applications to Modeling, Analysis, and Design of Systems in Medicine and Engineering, volume 19(3) of International Journal of Applied Mathematics and Computer Science. University of Zielona Gora Press (2009)
11. Schlesinger, S.: Terminology for Model Credibility. Simulation 32 (3), 103–104 (1979)
12. Tändl, M.,Stark, T., Erol, N., Löer, F., and Kecskeméthy, A.: An integrated simulation environment for human gait analysis and evaluation, Proceedings of the 10th International Symposium on Biomaterials: Fundamentals and Clinical Applications, Essen, Germany (2008)

Probabilistic Models with Uncertainty

Gabor Rebner
Department of Computer Science and Applied Cognitive Sciences
University of Duisburg-Essen
rebner@inf.uni-due.de

This talk addresses the research and development of stochastic models with uncertainty by utilizing intervals. The Dempster-Shafer theory (DST) is a tried and tested resource for this research project. It allows not just the definition of uncertain variables as intervals, but also assigns a mass to every piece of evidence. Through the identification of the evidence and its credibility, the engineer is shown options for how to compute stochastic models on modern computer systems using verified DST methods. Two elements contribute to the higher validity of these models: the intuitive definition of individual models and the possibility of modeling probability distributions with uncertainties.

One reason for the attractiveness of this field of study is the distinction between two kinds of uncertainties. The modeling of stochastic systems knows both aleatoric and epistemic uncertainties. This talk deals with both. Two examples of aleatoric uncertainties are uncertain failure probabilities in fault trees and uncertain probabilities in Markov chains. Where applicable, these models will be extended in the area of verified computations.

In the course of this talk, the combination of verified interval arithmetic and DST will be explored. The result of this effort is the Dempster-Shafer with Intervals (DSI) Toolbox for MATLAB, which, for the first time, offers support for the verified computer-based modeling and simulation of processes from different fields of application (with due consideration of aleatoric and epistemic uncertainties). Furthermore, the DSI Toolbox allows more accurate results for larger systems in a shorter time with the same hardware configuration (through parallelization on the graphics processing unit). An additional advantage is that one can work with an affordable system, thus reaching a large audience.

To achieve the described goals, the definitions of both the requirements for the reliability of numerical results and the mathematical methods will be given first. Then, we will take functions from C-XSC, which provides the ability to verify results, in order to discuss the extensions of MATLAB and INTLAB. With that in mind, we can continue to carry out the research, development, and implementation of probability algorithms that describe stochastic processes. We will discuss the optimization and verification of existing and newly developed software. This leads to a currently unique combination of verified stochastic fault tree analysis and high-performance computing (based on customary graphic processing units). The presentation concludes with an example of verified uncertain GPS localization based on the DST.

Probabilistic models with uncertainty

Dipl.-Inform. Gabor Rebner

University of Duisburg-Essen
Computer and Cognitive Sciences (INKO)
Duisburg, Germany

29.08.2013

Table Of Contents

Nomenclature

$\mathbb{R}$ Set of real numbers

$\mathbb{M}$ Set of floating-point numbers

$\mathbb{IR}$ Set of real-valued intervals

$\mathbb{IM}$ Set of floating-point intervals

$x,\ y,\ z$ Interval element of $\mathbb{IR}$ or $\mathbb{IM}$

$\mathbf{fl}_{\bigtriangledown}(a)$ Rounding of $a \in \mathbb{R}$ to the next floating-point number smaller than a

$\mathbf{fl}_{\bigtriangleup}(a)$ Rounding of $a \in \mathbb{R}$ to the next floating-point number greater than a

Definition: verification

Definition
We use the term verification in its narrow sense of providing mathematical proofs that the solution obtained on modern computer systems is correct.

Motivation

Modeling of polymorphic uncertainty

- ► Verified computation
  - ► Use of verified software libraries
    - ► INTLAB and C-XSC
- ► A broad range of applications
- ► Utilizing common software and hardware
- ► Wherever possible:
  - ► Utilizing costfree software
  - ► Easy handling

Example – Speed of GPS signals
$V_{GPS} \in [299704943, 299792458] \frac{m}{s}$

Modelling

Definition
Finite mapping of a real-life system, which can be deterministically solved on modern computer systems.

Definition from Wikipedia
Scientific modelling is a scientific activity with the goal of making a particular part or feature of the world easier to understand, define, quantify, visualize, or simulate.

Examples
Fault trees and Markov set-chains

What is uncertainty?

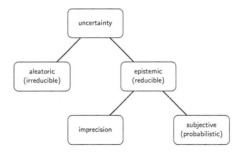

Figure: Definition of uncertainty (according to [1])

Modelling of uncertainty

Polymorphic uncertainty

- ► Fuzzy
  - ► Numbers
  - ► Intervals
- ► Intervals (Dempster-Shafer Theory)
- ► Deterministic values

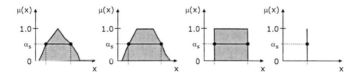

Figure: Polymorphic uncertainty. Extracted from [2]

Propagation of uncertainty

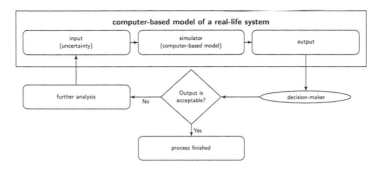

Figure: Propagation of uncertainty (according to [1])

IEEE standard for floating-point arithmetic

We utilize (defined by the IEEE 754-2008 standard)

- Definition and presentation of floating-point numbers
- Arithmetic operations and the corresponding failure
- Rounding operations.

Rounding operations

Applied rounding

- Rounding upwards $(y = \mathbf{fl}_\triangle (x) \mid x \in \mathbb{R}, y \in \mathbb{M})$
- Rounding downwards $(y = \mathbf{fl}_\triangledown (x) \mid x \in \mathbb{R}, y \in \mathbb{M})$

P1788 – Draft of an interval standard

The draft includes

- Definition and presentation of intervals on modern computer systems
  - Here: floating-point numbers in double precision
- Rounding operations
- Arithmetic operations on intervals

Intervals

Real-valued intervals $\mathbb{IR}$

$$x = [\underline{x}, \overline{x}] \mid \underline{x} \le x \le \overline{x} \text{ with } x \in \mathbb{R}$$

Machine interval $\mathbb{IM}$

$$y - [\underline{y}, \overline{y}] \mid \underline{y} \le y \le \overline{y} \text{ with } y \in \mathbb{M}$$

Zero-width interval

$$z = [\underline{z}, \overline{z}] \mid \underline{z} = z = \overline{z} \text{ with } z \in \mathbb{M}$$

DST – motivation

Initial position
Experts give uncertain evidences

Theory

- Belief variable: $\tilde{X}$
- Basic probability assignment (BPA): $\boldsymbol{A}$
  - Focal element from $\boldsymbol{A}$: $\boldsymbol{A}_i$
  - Mass assignment of $\boldsymbol{A}_i$: $m(\boldsymbol{A}_i)$

BPA

Basic Probability Assignment (BPA)

$$m : 2^{\tilde{X}} \to x \in [0,1] \text{ with } x \in \mathbb{R}$$

$$\sum_{i=1}^{n} m(\boldsymbol{A}_i) = 1$$

$$m(\emptyset) = 0$$

Graphical representation

$$PL\,(Y) := \sum_{A_i \cap Y \neq \emptyset} (m(A_i)), \;\; BEL\,(Y) := \sum_{A_i \subseteq Y} (m(A_i)) \text{ with } Y \subseteq \tilde{X}$$

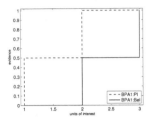

Normalization

Initial problem
Experts ignore the restrictions of the definition of a BPA
(Sum of mass $= 1$)

Verified normalization

$$m(A_i) \;\boxed{\div}\; \mathsf{fl}_\triangle \left(\sum_{j=1}^{n} m(A_j) \right), \;\;\; m(A_i) \;\boxed{\div}\; \mathsf{fl}_\triangledown \left(\sum_{j=1}^{n} m(A_j) \right)$$

Interoperability – definition and motivation

Definition
Interoperability is the ability of diverse systems and organizations
to work together (inter-operate). [Wikipedia]

Extension

- ▸ Expending the allocatable verified algorithms
- ▸ Expending the functionality of the observed program

The MEX Interface

The MEX Interface

- ► Direct access to the memory of MATLAB
  - ► No conversion failure
  - ► Fastest possibility
- ► C++ code is directly compiled in MATLAB
- ► Direct execution in MATLAB

Features

- ► A huge amount of (non-)verified algorithms to deal with polymorphic uncertainty
  - ► DST algorithms
  - ► Sampling of CDFs and (non-)monotonic system functions
  - ► Fault tree analysis with uncertainty
  - ► Markov set-chains (MSC)
  - ► ...
- ► Based on INTLAB and C-XSC
- ► Free download after registration (www.udue.de/DSI)

Interval-valued Basic Probability Assignment (IBPA)

Definition
Extension of a BPA with interval-valued mass assignments

$$m : 2^{\tilde{X}} \to x \in [0,1] \text{ with } x \in \mathbb{IM}$$

$$1 \in \sum_{i=1}^{n} m(A_i)$$

$$m(\emptyset) = [+0, +0]$$

Markov set-chains – The uncertain transition matrix

Uncertain transition matrix M
Defined by two real-valued matrices with dimension $n \times n$:

$$M_{ij} = [P_{ij}, Q_{ij}] \text{ with } P_{ij}, \ Q_{ij} \in \mathbb{M}$$

$$1 \in \sum_{i=1}^{n} M_{ij}$$

for all i, j=1,...,n.

Markov set-chains – the initial distribution

Uncertain initial distribution μ
Defined by two real-valued row-vectors with dimension n:

$$\mu_i = [p_i, q_i] \text{ with } p_i, \ q_i \in \mathbb{M}$$

$$1 \in \sum_{i=1}^{n} \mu_i$$

for all i=1,...,n.

Solution space

Definition
The solution space is defined by the cut set of the hyperplane defined by the unit vectors and the hypercube defined by the uncertain distribution.

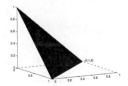

Figure: Stochastic vectors in $\mathbb{R}^3$

both pictures according to [1]

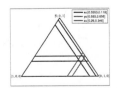

Figure: Example of a solution space

Implemented algorithms

Algorithms

- Test of a closed solution space
- Computation of a closed solution space
- Computation of the transition matrix for step $k \to k+1$
- Computation of the uncertain distribution in step k
- Computation of the uncertain coefficient of ergodicity

Fixed-point

- No fixed-point is available because of the outward rounding operations.

Fault tree analysis – graphical representation

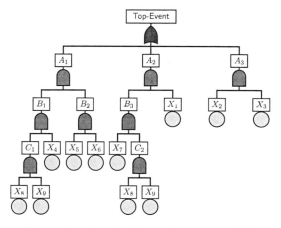

Figure: Example of a fault tree (according to [1])

Input

Scale

- Splitting the interval [0,1] in a course and a fine scale
  - Number of intervals in the course scale: $n - f$
  - Number of intervals in the fine scale: $f \cdot l$
  - Total count of intervals: $n - f + f \cdot l$
- For example $A := \{A_i\} \mid i = 1 \ldots n - f + f \cdot l$

Constraints

- No disjoint intervals are available in software
- Considerable time consumption by the computation of the logical gates

Input

Mass assignment

- ▸ Mass assignment is analogously defined to the Dempster-Shafer theory
- ▸ Initial problem:
  - ▸ Normalization after computation of logical gates
  - ▸ Over- or under-estimation of the masses after computation
- ▸ Advantage:
  - ▸ Any kind of mass assignment is possible

Uncertain failure distribution at the top event

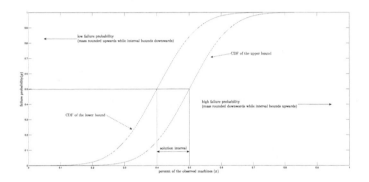

Figure: Computation of the uncertain failure distribution at the top event (according to [1])

AND-GATE

Lower bound

$$LB_{ij} = \mathbf{fl}_\triangledown \left(\underline{\boldsymbol{X}}_{\mathrm{i}} \cdot \underline{\boldsymbol{Y}}_{\mathrm{j}} \right)$$

$$\boldsymbol{m}(LB_{ij}) = \mathbf{fl}_\triangle \left(\overline{\boldsymbol{m}}(\boldsymbol{X}_{\mathrm{i}}) \cdot \overline{\boldsymbol{m}}(\boldsymbol{Y}_{\mathrm{j}}) \right)$$

Upper bound

$$UB_{ij} = \mathbf{fl}_\triangle \left(\overline{\boldsymbol{X}}_{\mathrm{i}} \cdot \overline{\boldsymbol{Y}}_{\mathrm{j}} \right)$$

$$\boldsymbol{m}(UB_{ij}) = \mathbf{fl}_\triangledown \left(\underline{\boldsymbol{m}}(\boldsymbol{X}_{\mathrm{i}}) \cdot \underline{\boldsymbol{m}}(\boldsymbol{Y}_{\mathrm{j}}) \right)$$

OR-GATE

Lower bound

$$LB_{ij} = \mathbf{fl}_\triangledown \left(\mathbf{fl}_\triangledown \left(\underline{X}_i + \underline{Y}_j \right) - \mathbf{fl}_\triangle \left(\underline{X}_i \cdot \underline{Y}_j \right) \right)$$
$$m(LB_{ij}) = \mathbf{fl}_\triangle \left(\overline{m}(X_i) \cdot \overline{m}(Y_j) \right)$$

Upper bound

$$UB_{ij} = \mathbf{fl}_\triangle \left(\mathbf{fl}_\triangle \left(\overline{X}_i + \overline{Y}_j \right) - \mathbf{fl}_\triangledown \left(\overline{X}_i \cdot \overline{Y}_j \right) \right)$$
$$m(UB_{ij}) = \mathbf{fl}_\triangledown \left(\underline{m}(X_i) \cdot \underline{m}(Y_j) \right)$$

Solution

x	$LB_{Traczinski}$	$UB_{Traczinski}$	LB_{new}	UB_{new}
0.05	$1.48 \cdot 10^{-4}$	$1.6 \cdot 10^{-4}$	$1.\overline{3} \cdot 10^{-4}$	$1.5\overline{6} \cdot 10^{-4}$
0.16	$3.6 \cdot 10^{-4}$	$3.74 \cdot 10^{-4}$	$3.4 \cdot 10^{-4}$	$3.7 \cdot 10^{-4}$
0.25	$5.6 \cdot 10^{-4}$	$5.76 \cdot 10^{-4}$	$5.3\overline{6} \cdot 10^{-4}$	$5.7 \cdot 10^{-4}$
0.38	$9.46 \cdot 10^{-4}$	$9.68 \cdot 10^{-4}$	$9.1\overline{6} \cdot 10^{-4}$	$9.5\overline{6} \cdot 10^{-4}$
0.45	$1.224 \cdot 10^{-3}$	$1.248 \cdot 10^{-3}$	$1.19 \cdot 10^{-3}$	$1.23\overline{6} \cdot 10^{-3}$
0.84	$7.58 \cdot 10^{-3}$	$7.63 \cdot 10^{-3}$	$7.47 \cdot 10^{-3}$	$7.56 \cdot 10^{-3}$
0.95	$2.78 \cdot 10^{-2}$	$2.84 \cdot 10^{-2}$	$2.68 \cdot 10^{-2}$	$2.82 \cdot 10^{-2}$
E	no information	no information	$7.481 \cdot 10^{-3}$	$7.632 \cdot 10^{-3}$

Complexity

Gates
Find the minima of the functions:

$$\text{OR-GATE}: p_1 + \frac{n}{p_1}$$
$$\text{AND-GATE}: p_2 + \frac{2n}{p_2}$$

Let n be the number of elements in the scale and p_i the number of partitions of the scale.

▶ Solution
  ▸ $p_1 = \sqrt{n}$
  ▸ $p_2 = \sqrt{2 \cdot n}$

Compute Unified Device Architecture (CUDA)

CUDA

- ▶ Software library by NVIDIA
- ▶ Massive parallelization on the Graphics Processing Unit (GPU)
- ▶ Directed rounding operations defined by IEEE754 in double format
- ▶ Free download at http://www.nvidia.com
- ▶ Executable on consumer GPUs

Example of the optimization

Let X and Y be two scales with nine interval elements.

$$\mathbf{fl}_{\triangledown}\left(\mathbf{fl}_{\triangledown}\left(\underline{X}_3 + \underline{Y}_4\right) - \mathbf{fl}_{\triangle}\left(\underline{X}_3 \cdot \underline{Y}_4\right)\right)$$

$$\mathbf{fl}_{\triangledown}\left(\mathbf{fl}_{\triangledown}\left(\underline{X}_6 + \underline{Y}_7\right) - \mathbf{fl}_{\triangle}\left(\underline{X}_6 \cdot \underline{Y}_7\right)\right)$$

1,1	1,2	1,3	1,4	1,5	1,6	1,7	1,8	1,9
2,1	2,2	2,3	2,4	2,5	2,6	2,7	2,8	2,9
3,1	3,2	3,3	3,4	3,5	3,6	3,7	3,8	3,9
4,1	4,2	4,3	4,4	4,5	4,6	4,7	4,8	4,9
5,1	5,2	5,3	5,4	5,5	5,6	5,7	5,8	5,9
6,1	6,2	6,3	6,4	6,5	6,6	6,7	6,8	6,9
7,1	7,2	7,3	7,4	7,5	7,6	7,7	7,8	7,9
8,1	8,2	8,3	8,4	8,5	8,6	8,7	8,8	8,9
9,1	9,2	9,3	9,4	9,5	9,6	9,7	9,8	9,9

Figure: Graphical representation of the parallelization utilizing the GPU (according to [1])

Solutions of the optimization

Table: Solutions in seconds. Extracted from [3]

	C++	C++ (new approach)
lower bound	505	71
upper bound	467	71

Motivation

Initial problems

- Defective GPS measurements
- Failure are defined by extrinsic and intrinsic characteristics:
  - Delay of the GPS signals (broadcasted by satellites)
  - Failure with the clock synchronization
  - Defective computation (logic of the sensor)
  - ...

Extension of the DST to two dimensions

Approach

Extending the DST with two dimensional IBPAs.

2DIBPA

Definition

$$m : 2^{\tilde{X}} \to x \in [0, 1] \text{ with } x \in \mathbb{IM}$$

$$1 \in \sum_{i=1}^{n} m(A_i), \ m(\emptyset) = [+0, +0]$$

$$m(A_i) = [+0, +0], \text{ if } A_{i_x} = \emptyset \text{ or } A_{i_y} = \emptyset$$

2DIBPA – graphical representation

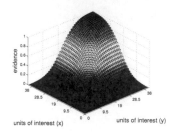

Figure: CDF of a 2D normal distribution [3]

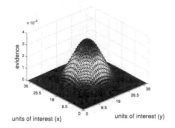

Figure: PDF of a 2D normal distribution [3]

Referenzen

Rebner, G.:

Intervallbasierte Berechnungsverfahren zur Beschreibung von wahrscheinlichkeitstheoretischen Modellen mit Unsicherheit. first edn.

Verlag Dr. Hut, Munich (2013) graduate thesis at the University of Duisburg-Essen – ISBN 978-3-8439-1283-9.

Graf, W.:

Safety and robustness assessment of structures with polymorphic uncertainty.

Talk for the FP7-ITN (2012)

Rebner, G., Sacher, D., Luther, W.:

Verified stochastic methods: The evolution of the Dempster-Shafer with intervals (DSI) toolbox.

In Deodatis, G., Ellingwood, B., Frangopol, D., eds.: Safety, Reliability, Risk and Life-Cycle Performance of Structures and Infrastructures, CRC Press (Juni 2013) 98 published abstract.

Building Suitability Maps Using Incomplete and Uncertain Context Information

Jonathan Frez[1] Nelson Baloian[2], Gustavo Zurita[3]

[1] School of Informatics and Telecommunications, Universidad Diego Portales
Jonathan.frez@gmail.com
[2] Department of Computer Science, Universidad de Chile
nbaloian@dcc.uchile.cl
[3] Management Control and Information Systems Department, Universidad de Chile
gzurita@fen.uchile.cl

Abstract. Although geographic information systems (GISs) have been extensively used by decision makers when dealing with location-related issues, few of them provide the functionalities needed to support the classic decision-making process. This process consists in identifying the problem, modeling the situation, and then generating a series of scenarios based on various hypotheses and evaluating them until a satisfactory solution to the problem has been identified. In this paper, we present a system that abstracts the modeling, minimizes the GIS knowledge needed, and generates multiple scenarios, enabling decision makers to compare them easily.

Keywords: Decision making, GIS, Dempster-Shafer, Decision support systems

Decision support systems (DSS) have been defined as interactive computer-based systems that assist decision makers in using data and models to solve unstructured problems. A simplified model for the decision-making process (DM) includes the following stages: 1) identifying the problem, 2) identifying and modeling the objective(s) of the decision, 3) collecting, generating, and/or combining data to generate alternative scenarios, 4) evaluating alternatives based on the objectives established, and 5) choosing an alternative and conducting a sensitive analysis. If decision maker(s) estimate(s) there is enough information, the process ends with a final decision; otherwise, the flow returns to step 2, identifying objectives, or to step 3, generating alternatives (see Fig 1). As for artificial intelligence, the boundaries for defining what constitutes DSS seem diffuse. However, most authors who have tried to define DSS agree that one of the most important characteristics is that human judgment remains a key factor in the decision-making process, generating alternatives and redefining and remodeling objectives, since this is a task involving creativity, which cannot be mechanized. Computers, in turn, can help humans gather data, generate various decision alternatives, evaluate the outcome of these alternatives based on predefined goals, visualize the results, and communicate the results to others.

GIS technology is often used to support DMs for which intensive use of geo-referenced information is needed in order to generate and evaluate the outcomes of the various alternative scenarios. These kinds of DMs involve, among other activities, generating a large set of alternatives, each with multiple evaluation criteria.

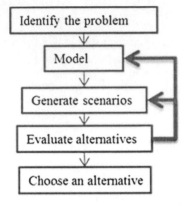

Fig. 1 The decision-making process [1]

From the available literature about GISs being used to support DM, we realize that there are a significant number of modeling tools available that can generate a scenario for a geographical area, apply certain evaluation functions, and show the output, like the winter survival of vegetation [2], wind farm locations [3], or estimations of forest production [4]. However, the great majority of the existing GISs are not explicitly designed to implement a DM cycle, which means that the process of generating various alternative scenarios according to different criteria and comparing them is, in most cases, a difficult and time consuming task. In order to implement a DM process, we need to abstract the modeling step from the DM cycle and allow the decision maker to generate multiple scenarios and compare the solutions in a simple and systematic way.

For example, one of the most common uses of a GIS as a DSS is finding a **suitable area**, given some requirement. For example, [5] explains how to find specific locations for constructing artificial water-recharge aquifers using floods. The DM in a suitability decision seems to follow a pattern: The decision maker is an expert on the decision criteria (in this case, aquifer recharge), but is not necessarily an expert in GIS. Historical information is needed, which can easily be represented using GISs. A suitability criteria/formula is then designed by the decision maker, and the criteria is used for formulating a query to the GIS. A **suitability map** is then returned showing the suitability level of each point on the map to satisfy a requirement.

Using a GIS as a DSS has two main problems. First, one hypothesis of what area may be suitable is represented by the criteria/formula, and one map is returned; thus, the decision maker makes the decision based on a single scenario generated by a single hypothesis. Second, it is hard to evaluate the impact of changing the hypothesis because, in order to generate another alternative, a new "project" must be created, configured, computed, and finally evaluated. In order to create multiple alternatives, the decision maker must create multiple maps and compare them. However, most GISs are designed to create maps, not to compare them, or to make decisions based on multiple alternative maps generated from varying criteria.

This paper presents a software design and prototype that allows build scenarios for decision making, abstracting the modeling, minimizing the GIS knowledge needed, and allowing several scenarios to be built and easily compared. This is accomplished by applying Dempster-Shafer theory to GIS data. Dempster-Shafer theory is a mathematical framework for decision making.

References

1. Antunes, P., Sapateiro, C., Zurita, G., and Baloian, N.: Integrating Spatial Data and Decision Models in an E-planning Tool. Collaboration and Technology, Springer, 297–112 (2010)
2. Ouellet, C., and Sherk, L.: Woody Ornamental Plant Zonation: III. Suitability Map for the Probable Winter Survival of Ornamental Trees and Shrubs. Canadian Journal of Plant Science 47 (4), 351–358 (1967)
3. Baban, S. M., and Parry, T.: Developing and Applying a GIS-assisted Approach to Locating Wind Farms in the UK. Renewable Energy 24 (1), 59–71 (2001)
4. Ekanayake, G., and Dayawansa, N.: Land Suitability Identification for a Production Forest through GIS Techniques. Department of Agricultural Engineering, Faculty of Agriculture, University of Peradeniya, Peradeniya Sri Lanka. Map India Conference (2003)
5. Ghayoumian, J., Ghermezcheshme, B., Feiznia S., and Noroozi, A., A.: Integrating GIS and DSS for Identification of Suitable Areas for Artificial Recharge, Case Study Meimeh Basin, Isfahan, Iran. Environmental Geology 47 (4), 493–500 (2005)

SDSS

Spatial Decision Support Systems & Fuzzy modeling &
Belief functions

DSS

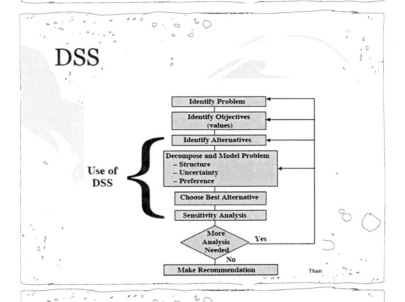

Use of DSS

SDSS

- Geometries

SDSS

- Geometries
- Scale/Area

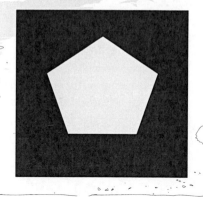

SDSS

- Geometries
- Scale/Area
- Atributes&Values

5 persons/m2

90'

Multicriteria decision models into GIS

- Boolean techniques of MCDM
- Multiple alternatives
- Objective function
- The only accurate storage can be one-to-one scale

00

Fuzzy logic & multicriteria evaluations

○ indeterminate boundaries
○ Combining fuzzy sets
○ fuzzy measures
○ **Several specific scenarios**
  ■ Forest insect infestations
  ■ Priority sites for marine protection
  ■ Environmental models
  ■ Environmental vulnerability

fuzzy boundaries

10'

Analysis that allows continuous or fuzzy functions

- dynamic generation of maps (impact of parameters)
- decision making process
- models
- fuzzy generation of geographic information (by models)
- Suitability Maps
  ○ Cells evaluation of objective function

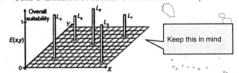

Keep this in mind

Continuous or fuzzy functions

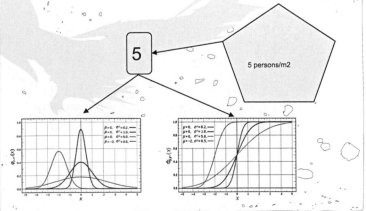

5

5 persons/m2

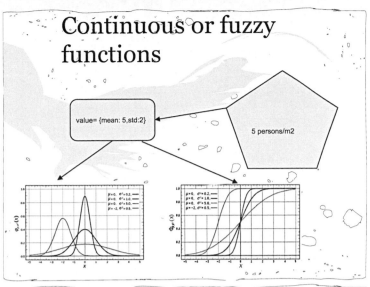

Continuous or fuzzy functions

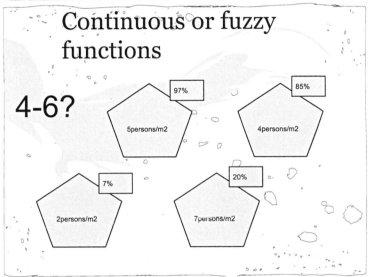

Continuous or fuzzy functions

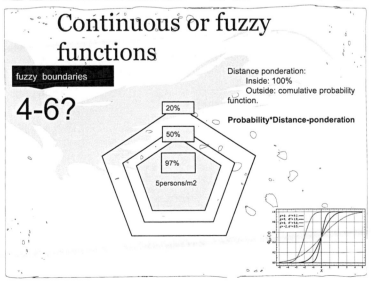

Continuous or fuzzy functions

Problems

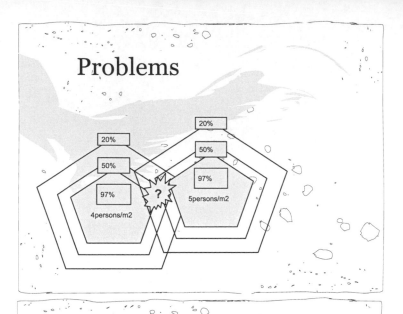

Problems

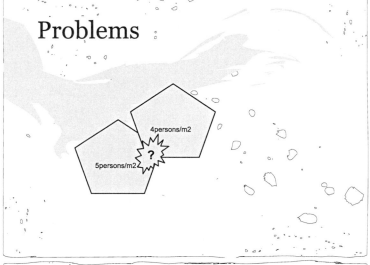

Problem examples

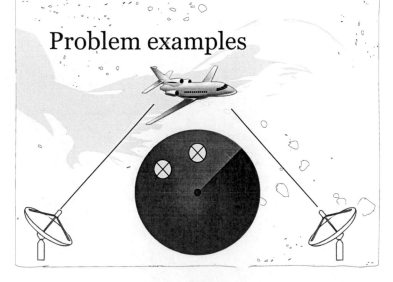

Problem examples

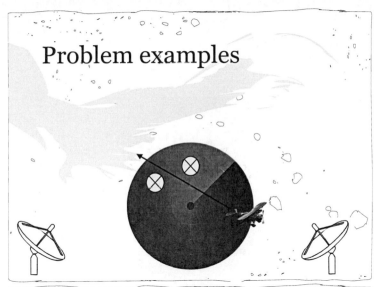

Problem Example

60km in the
sea

Dempster–Shafer theory

Allows to combine evidence from different
sources and arrive at a degree of belief.

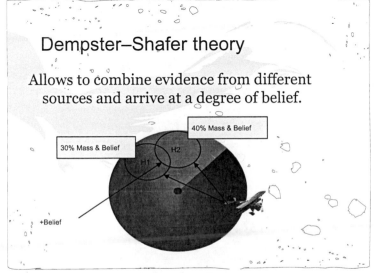

40% Mass & Belief

30% Mass & Belief

H2

H1

+Belief

Experiments

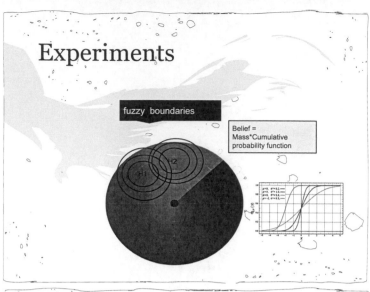

Experiments

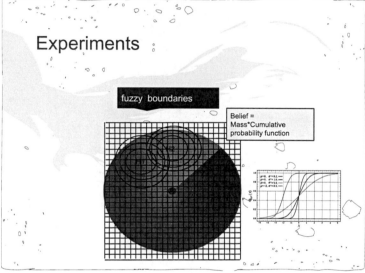

Experiments

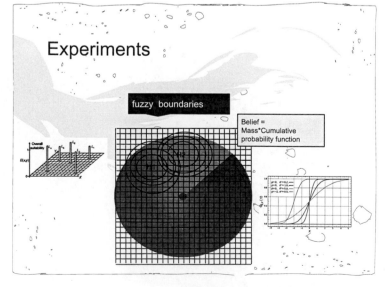

Experiments

Goodchild(1990) all features stored in a GIS are inherently fuzzy and uncertain.

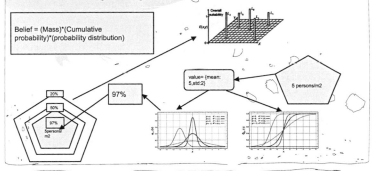

Belief = (Mass)*(Cumulative probability)*(probability distribution)

value= (mean: 5,std:2)

5 persons/m2

97%

20%

50%

97%

5persons/m2

Belief +fuzzy boundaries + continuous functions

Experiments

However....
Constraints...

people don't walk on the water.... (Jesus does not count).

We need types & rules..
Ontology ---> Interaction between classes.

ex:
people on water... no.
water on people... yes.

Experiment 01

Experiment 01

SDSS

Parameters:

- Mass or Belief of the sources.
- std,mean or parameters for the probability function(s).

Types -> Classes -> Ontology

SDSS

Classes

- " There are people near/inside commercial areas, schools, and churches".
  - People -> distribution.
  - H1: Commercial : Mass 40%.
  - H2: Schools: Mass 30%.
  - H3: Churches: 10%.
  - H4 : Commercial +Schools+Churches.

Experiment 02

OpenStreetMap -> Database ->Basic Ontology of elements.

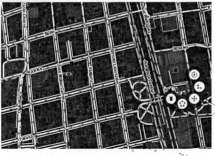

Experiment 02

1.1 Aerialway	1.10.3 Lifecycle	2.5.4 Discount store, charity
1.2 Aeroway	1.10.4 Attributes	2.5.5 Health and Beauty
1.3 Amenity	1.10.5 Other features	2.5.6 Do-it-yourself, household goods, building materials, gardening products
1.3.1 Sustenance	1.11 Historic	
1.3.2 Education	1.12 Landuse	2.5.7 Furniture and Interior
1.3.3 Transportation	1.13 Leisure	2.5.8 Electronics
1.3.4 Financial	1.14 Man Made	2.5.9 Outdoors and Sport, Vehicles
1.3.5 Healthcare	1.15 Military	2.5.10 Art, music, hobbies
1.3.6 Entertainment, Arts & Culture	1.16 Natural	2.5.11 Stationery, gifts, books, newspapers
1.3.7 Others	1.17 Office	
1.4 Barrier	1.18 Places	2.5.12 Others
1.5 Boundary	2.1 Power	2.6 Sport
1.6 Building	2.2 Public Transport	2.7 Tourism
1.7 Craft	2.3 Railway	2.8 Waterway
1.8 Emergency	2.4 Route	
1.9 Geological	2.5 Shop	
1.10 Highway	2.5.1 Food, Beverages	
1.10.1 Roads	2.5.2 General store, department store, mall	
1.10.2 Paths	2.5.3 Clothing, shoes, accessories	

Experiment 02

H1 -> People are in shops 60% (40% means nothing)

Santiago -> spatial objects in the database +500.000

10x10 grid at max zoom. -> 300.000 distance evaluations (fuzzy boundaries).

Experiment 02

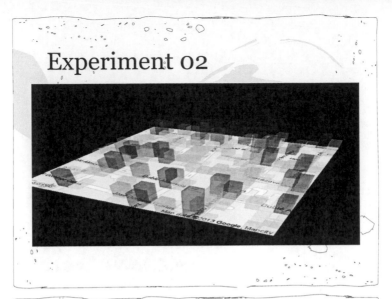

Performance

PostGIS
Node.js
REST calls

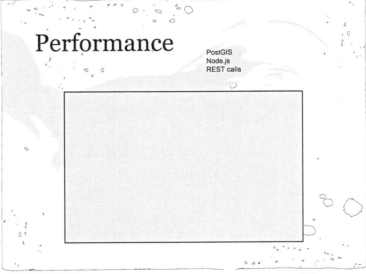

Performance

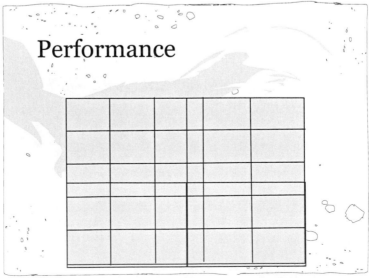

Performance

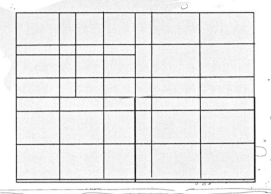

Performance

Quad processing tree

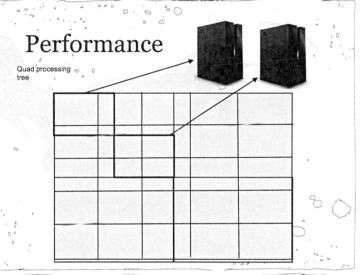

Future work

- Problems with the combination rules of Dempster-Shafer Theory
- Combine hypothesis (shops+schools, etc).
- Time dependent modeling (schools)
- Method to specify:
  - Constraints
  - Grid resolutions
  - Models (continuous functions & fuzzy boundaries)
  - **DSS process.**